SNUFF
YESTERDAY AND TODAY

by

C. W. SHEPHERD

CONTENTS

Introduction		9
I	Snuff's Lively History	17
II	The Elegant Age	25
III	Snuff in the Making	35
IV	A Guide to Snuff Varieties	40
V	Snuff-taking Today	48
VI	The Lure of the Snuff-box	53
VII	Snuff-taking Ladies	65
VIII	Snuff and Health	72
IX	Snuff in Story and Song	78

To
VIVIAN ROSE
of
Smith's Snuff Shop
For Help So
Freely Given

ILLUSTRATIONS

A snuff-blender's sign	*facing page*	16
Modern snuff packaging		16
The old shop in Charing Cross Road		17
Old bone snuff-taking spoon and antique snuff-rasp		32
Mechanical snuff-grinding pestle and mortar and ancient water-wheel		33
A selective customer		48
Modern snuff-boxes and a Royal gift		49
Snuff-boxes		64
Snuff-taking ladies		65

INTRODUCTION

*"Whate'er I do; where'er I be,
My social box attends on me."*
REV. WILLIAM KING, 1788.

THE general conception of a revolution is of something which goes off with a bang. But there is another kind of revolution which steals upon us almost before we are aware of it; it comes, as it were, with "the panther's velvet tread," and not with the charge of a buffalo. One such revolution is at work today; it is the quiet return of snuff-taking as a social habit.

Those who would dispute this should speak warily, for there is ample evidence lurking round the corner to confound them—the evidence of those whose business it is to mill, blend or sell snuff. Thus, there are blenders who, a decade ago, sold some hundreds of pounds weight of snuff annually, now measure their output—home and export—by the ton.

The increase in snuff-taking is not confined to men. More women are taking to the "tobacco powder," as it was once called (and which it is), thus reviving the vogue snuff had among the ladies of the eighteenth century and later. The famous blenders, G. Smith and Sons, of Charing Cross Road, will tell us that an increasing proportion of their customers today are women. The subject of Women and Snuff is dealt with in Chapter VII.

It is difficult to analyse the general return to favour of snuff-taking; some say the enormous rise in the price of tobacco and cigarettes is the reason; certainly, by comparison, snuff-taking is a most economical pleasure. The cigarette "scare" naturally bumped up snuff sales for a time, but it had little to do with the steady increase which is progressing all the time. There are other possible reasons, but we will leave them to emerge in their appropriate chapters in this book.

One of the fascinations of snuff-taking lies in the numerous different snuffs available to the snuff-taker. The mellow old firm of Smith and Sons—known as "Smith's of Charing Cross Road" to thousands of snuff-takers the world over—produce at least fifty varieties of snuffs from choice tobaccos whose broad leaves have ripened in sunnier climes than ours, and many of these snuffs are described in detail in Chapter IV.

To those who think of snuff as "just snuff" the number of varieties comes as a surprise, and their picturesque names perhaps a revelation. Who can fail to be charmed by such appellations as Golden Cardinal, Lavender and Otterburn, not to mention Garden Mint, an innovation of Smith's, with a distinct whiff of real mint about it? There are, too, the "natural" snuffs, with no flavouring save that of honest-to-goodness tobacco. And here it may be mentioned that, basically, snuff consists of nothing else; the addition of other substances except flavouring being prohibited by law. Long gone are the days when dried and powdered dock leaves and other substances were craftily mixed with the tobacco.

SNUFF FRIENDSHIPS

In the diversity of snuffs lies much of snuff's *social* success, for one of the pleasures of exchanging a pinch is to discover what kind of snuff the other fellow uses, and to compare its merits or demerits with our own. Many friendships are formed by this genial practice. The traditional aloofness of the Englishman to strangers disappears at the proffering of a snuff-box by one man to another who, he has noticed, takes a pinch himself.

"Thank you, sir, I shall be delighted," says the invitee; then, after taking a sniff with a discriminating look, he will say something like this:

"Ah, that's very good. I should says there's a touch of Latakia in it?"

"Quite right," comes the answer, "it's Spanish with a trace of Latakia, as you said. I always add a little to my snuffs. A touch of the Middle East, you know."

And then the two will get down to comparing their respective snuff-boxes, for the box is often as worthy of a chat as the snuff inside it. The pair, having, as one might say, become snuff-brothers, will recognise each other if they chance to meet again, and will at once offer each other a friendly pinch, even if it means crossing the saloon bar to do it!

As for snuff-boxes, these are always a quiet joy to their owners, for most of them possess a definite individuality, as well as often disclosing the individuality of their owners. Many snuff-takers possess quite a variety of boxes, picked up here and there, or given to them as presents by understanding intimates. They thus become collectors, albeit in only a minor way. Collecting snuff-boxes in the real sense can be a profitable as well as an entertaining hobby. There is always the possibility of a surprise, though not so thrilling as one which occurred recently at Sotheby's auction rooms when the auctioneer put up a snuff-box and saw the bidding rise to 2,000 guineas before he brought down his hammer. Valuable it was known to be; but 2,000 guineas! It might have been a racehorse. (The reason for the value of this box will be found on a later page.)

The beauties of the snuff-box did not vanish with the gold and diamond specimens of the Louis XIV period in France and the Regency days here. Many choice examples are made by craftsmen today, and are obtainable at uncommonly reasonable prices. Today's specimens are made mostly of silver, pewter, horn or rosewood, and Smith's makes a speciality of putting these boxes before the public. (See Chapter V. —The Lure of the Snuff-box.)

NO ORDINARY SHOP

The fascinating history of snuff, going back beyond the days of Raleigh, is examined closely in our first two chapters.

The health value of snuff is nowadays under consideration, and it is increasingly prescribed by doctors for those who work in a dusty atmosphere, or who suffer from certain complaints. We shall take a look at these matters later on. (Chapter VIII.)

The history of Smith's Snuff Shop, as it is widely called, must claim a few words in this Introduction, for it is no ordinary shop.

It looks exactly as it did close on a hundred years ago, when George Smith moved from the snuff-shop he had set up in the then unsalubrious area of Seven Dials nearby.

Should some chronicler ever attempt to write a book on shops and houses made famous by the numbers on their doors, he would not be short of examples, and would take in, of a certainly, No. 1 London, No. 10 Downing Street, and No. 48 Doughty Street, an old home of Dickens. Snuff-shops would undoubtedly come into his list with No. 37 Fleet Street and No. 74 Charing Cross Road. The former was the shop of John Hardham, whose snuff was so famous in the eighteenth century that it went by the name of " Thirty-seven," with no other description needed. Moreover, it had the advantage of rhyming with " heaven," which was a godsend to the snuff versifiers of the day—and there were plenty of them—as will be seen in our last chapter, " Snuff in Song and Story." Thus, one of them extolling a certain snuff:

> " This a treat is, this is my nose's heaven;
> This far exceeds old Hardham's 37."

True, he brought in old Hardham's name, but he need not have done. There was a Hardman shop—though not at 37—in Fleet Street until a few years ago. But this was long after the original Hardham had been called to his fathers, after which the business changed its address several times.

Our chronicler of historic street numbers will now have reached No. 74 Charing Cross Road, and this, in brief, is what he will find, though first of all he will consider the unique street in which the shop is located. There must be many who buy their Smith's snuffs without ever visiting the West-End, perhaps by post, or from some local tobacconist, who feel an occasional curiosity as to what kind of street is this Charing Cross Road. Their conceptions will differ; few, however, will imagine it as it is.

There is no street quite like it in the whole of London— or in the Provinces, either. Despite its proximity to the West-End's theatre-land, and to Trafalgar Square with its cosmopolitan pigeon-feeding crowds, there are few stretches in Charing Cross Road which do not breathe antiquity—not a very old antiquity, it is true, but one offering nearly a century of memories. Old second-hand bookshops abound, while some windows display—within and without—such quantities of old prints as to transport one back to the periods they depict.

BUYING A BOOK

The proprietors of these shops, like their forebears, have no objection to one browsing around as one is inclined. They know that your being there indicates interest, and that you are quite likely to fall for a book or print in the end. The late Arthur Ransome gave a charming sidelight on this in his book *Bohemia in London*. You have been browsing at the window, wondering whether to buy a book against the advice of your pocket. Then:

" . . . . At last you are conquered, and a book leads you

by the hand to the passionless little man inside the shop, and makes you pay him money—a sordid symbol that the book has won, and swayed the pendulum of your emotions past the paying point."

Ransome also tells a good story about the great book emporium, Foyle's, the biggest book shop in the world, which stands a little to the north of Smith's Snuff Shop, on the opposite side of " The Road." A customer, he says, once entered Foyle's and asked if they could let him have a book called " The Decline and Fall of the Holborn Empire."

The architectural history of Charing Cross Road is somewhat sketchy, for it more or less grew into a road as a result of old-time street alterations and name adjustments. Thus, one reads that Hog Lane, north of Seven Dials, became Crown Street, which became absorbed, by name at any rate, into Charing Cross Road, which itself, as such, dates only from 1886. But that in no way dates many of the shops.

Among these shops—the smallest and oldest-looking of them all—is No. 74, over which a sign proclaims it to be *Smith's Snuff Shop*.

In the window one sees a ripe assortment of age-browned tobacco-jars, pipes ancient and modern, snuff-boxes, cigars, loose tobaccos and yellowed prints reflecting the delights of smoking and snuff-taking. A statue of a Highlander taking snuff—once the true sign of the snuff-blender—looks out at us with the detachment of one who has known less sophisticated days than these.

To enter the shop is to pass into a world one fancied as gone. The pervading tone is russet brown, from the original pitted oaken counter with its brass hand-scales, the mellowed jars and snuff-canisters on the shelves, Even the walls are clothed with a friendly umber, and the prints which adorn them are tinted by the years. Overall, is the pervading fragrance of scores of different snuffs and loose tobaccos, here to be blended into mixtures, the secrets of which, one rightly thinks, belong to Smith's alone.

Further pleasure awaits the rarely privileged who step behind the counter into the old-fashioned premises behind, where the mysteries of blending hide themselves. It would be no surprise to see here the lean Uriah Heep of Dickens, seated at one of the well-worn desks, or, ignoring chronology for a moment, even the shade of the solid Dr. Johnson himself, ever and anon taking a pinch of snuff from a waistcoat pocket—leather-lined for the purpose, for he never used a snuff-box. One hears him saying:

" Sir, you may give your boxes to beaux and nincompoops. Snuff's the stuff, sir, and a plague on adornments."

A customary snuff-blender's trade-sign showing a Highlander taking a pinch

Snuff may be bought loose or in elegant little glass jars like these

The old shop in Charing Cross Road

CHAPTER I

Snuff's Lively History

*"Most rare Columbus; thou shalt be, for this,
The only Christopher in my kalendar.
Why but for thee the uses of the nose
Were half unknown, and its capacity
Of joy."*
                          OLD ANTHOLOGY.

IT is both laudable and typical of the English to credit the introduction of tobacco into Europe to one of their own countrymen, a gentleman by the name of Raleigh. This bit of " one-upmanship " has led Britishers of three centuries into the pleasant paths of self-deception. Yet even Sir Walter must have been quite aware that both tobacco and snuff were in use in Europe long before he set foot on American shores. We must not forget that Raleigh, apart from being a soldier, sailor and courtier, was a historian—not only of England, but of the World. He must also have had a remarkable memory, or he could not have written his *Historie of the World* during his imprisonment in the Tower of London, which doubtless did not include a reference library among its amenities.

As a historian he would naturally keep an eye on what was going on in the world " from India to Peru," and would have heard of a genial priest named Romano Pane who sailed with Christopher Columbus on his second voyage of discovery. It was he who discovered the Indians of the New World both smoking and snuffing tobacco.

With astonishment he noticed that the Indians took their tobacco in powdered form through a " Y "-shaped cane, the ends of " Y " being inserted in the nostrils, and the other in the tobacco dust, otherwise snuff. *This is the first recorded instance of the taking of snuff.* Even when it began to be used in Europe, the method of taking it was to dip a hollow cane or quill into the snuff and to transfer a " pinch " to the back of the hand for sniffing.

On his return to Spain, Romano told many stories of the Indians and their tobacco. Such stories were eagerly absorbed by the Spaniards, especially as Romano had stressed the medicinal value of the strange herb. But it was not every year, or every ten years that Spaniards sailed to Central America with its snuff-taking Indians. At length Philip the Second of Spain instructed one of his physicians, Francesco Hernandez, to visit Mexico and report on its natural productions. It is said that he brought back both leaves and seeds of the tobacco plant.

At that time the French Ambassador to Portugal was Jean Nicot, Lord of Villemain, and he was able to purchase some tobacco leaves brought into Portugal from neighbouring Spain. These he sent to Paris, some as a personal gift to Catherine de Medici, who was now the queen of Charles II of France, probably with instructions on powdering the leaves into snuff. Catherine tried it out, and thus perpetuated her name as the first woman to take snuff. Others—men and women—followed suit, to discover, naturally enough, that the taking of *tabac en poudre,* whatever its health virtues might be, was a pleasant indulgence. It was the Queen's patronage which thus set snuff going in France, though firstly only as a fashion with the Court.

WHO WAS FIRST?

As for Jean Nicot, about whom there is more in Chapter VII, his name will live forever in the word *Nicotine.* To discover the origin of the name *tobacco* is not so easy, and a search through various old volumes reveals much conflicting evidence. Because Columbus discovered the island of Tobago, many maintain this to have given birth to the name. It sounds likely enough until one reads that after Columbus and his faithful priest found the natives of San Domingo inhaling through their Y-pipe, which they called a *tobago* (or even a *tobaco*), he named the newly discovered island after it, because the island—or what part of it he could see, anyhow—suggested the shape of the snuff-pipe of the San Domingans.

It was many years after the introduction of tobacco into Europe that people began to *smoke*. Everyone was for snuff. Smoking was to come, but not yet. It is an oddity of tobacco history that the case was reversed when tobacco reached England, for smoking preceded snuffing by something like a century, by which time snuff began to oust the pipe, only to be ousted itself more than a century later, mainly by the cigarette. Just which way the cat is going to jump today is uncertain, but we have read in the Introduction to this book that snuff is on its way in again.

A piece of important history arises here; who first brought tobacco to England, and who first used it for smoking in a pipe? Never was anything so conflicting. If the history of tobacco in England were as well documented as its French record, this writer's world would have been a better place for a while! The reader might comment that, this being a book about snuff, why smoke the midnight pipe, and sniff the midnight pinch in search of elusive evidence? The reply is that tobacco, being the mother of snuff, merits all the attention we can give to its own lineage.

SIR WALTER'S IMAGE

Down the course of research, quite understandably, flits the inevitable image of Sir Walter Raleigh. But reference to many old books lead us to credit Raleigh only with being *the first "man of note"* to smoke and to encourage smoking. This was a long time after tobacco was introduced to the Continent. More than one authority says that Sir John Hawkins, the gallant admiral, brought tobacco to England, possibly from France, or perhaps direct from America. The great historian, Camden, gave the credit to that rollicking bandit, Sir Francis Drake, and so did the Scottish historian, David Hume. Others credit a Ralph Lane, governor of Raleigh's state, Virginia, with being the first to bring it here, and this seems likely enough to explain the legend which has clung so tenaciously to Raleigh.

Snuff-taking, like most enjoyable practices, naturally became a target for the kill-joys, and there was strong opposition to it abroad, and, later, in England. Snuff-taking became a well-practised habit among the clergy of the Continent. This roused the ire of Pope Urban VIII, and he set about eradicating it. In those days the priest would not begin his sermon or homily, or whatever it was then called, without first taking a hefty pinch of snuff. This he would repeat at intervals during his dissertation, particularly if he were momentarily stumped. The operation, if slightly prolonged, gave him time to think the thing out. It was not to be wondered at if his congregation did the same. So Urban frowned and put his foot down—both feet, in fact, for he interdicted the use of snuff altogether in places of worship.

But to stop this inoccuous pleasure was more easily said than done, especially as sermons sometimes lasted two or three hours, so that listeners needed something to keep them awake. Consequently the Pope merely won a half-victory. His successor, Pope Innocent, renewed the attack, but, as an old writer put it, he must have been very innocent indeed if he thought he could eradicate so simple a pleasure by such ponderous means.

OFF WITH HIS NOSE

Next to the attack a few years later was Sultan Amurath IV, who stepped up the penalty by making snuff-taking a capital offence, while in Russia the habit was forbidden under pain of the offender having his nose cut off. Of our own James I's attempts to stop smoking and snuffing we shall read in the next chapter. A good story is told of one of Louis XIII's tame physicians, who was instructed by his royal master to deliver a denunciation of snuff from a popular rostrum in Paris: and this at a time when snuff was taken by all classes of French society from " peasant to peacock," and when a man's affluence was often measured by the costliness of his snuff and snuff-box.

The physician's instructions were to impress his listeners with the fact that the Angel of Death lurked in every snuff-box. He was a good orator, and soon had his audience turning pale as, one by one, he described the grim diseases caused by snuff. In fact, so fervid did he become that he absent-mindedly produced his own jewelled snuff-box, tapped it, took a hearty pinch, paused portentously, then went on again. Needless to say, the pallor of his audience disappeared like dew before the sun's early rays.

There can be no certainty as to just how soon snuff-taking followed smoking in this country. It seems to have crept in somewhere around the Restoration, when Charles II returned from France, and even then its use was mainly confined to the well-to-do folk who had travelled abroad. And, of course, Charles was followed by a "tail" of French elegants, all of whom had their expensive snuffs and gold snuff-boxes. The "plebs" of this country, however, were not slow to imitate their betters, and we find them doing their best with snuffs quite unlike the refined and delicately perfumed varieties used by the gallants. Between Charles II's arrival in 1660, and 1665, the year of the Great Plague, snuff was taken by the masses in a more or less desultory manner;

but the horrors of the Plague quickly altered things. Distraught men looked everywhere for some kind of disinfectant to carry about with them when the sound of the death-cart's wheels was rarely out of their ears.

Many took to smoking, and, in old engravings, those engaged in burying the thousands of London's un-coffined dead are frequently shown with pipes in their mouths. Moreover, it became noticeable at the time that workers engaged in making or selling tobacco and snuff seemed to enjoy a good measure of security from the pestilence. This was full justification for the citizens to turn to snuff-taking, carrying the snuff with them in any small receptacle, so long as it had a lid. This led to the making of pathetically crude snuff-boxes, often by men who did not live to use them.

A SNUFF HAUL

After the Plague came the Great Fire in the next year, which did much to clear the air of London. During the following years snuff-taking remained with the people, but still on no great scale. One reason for this was that snuff was not easy to obtain in quantities except by the richer classes. Then came an incident in the War of the Spanish Succession, in full swing about the year 1702, which suddenly made snuff an easily obtainable commodity. Admiral Sir George Rooke had set out with a combined fleet of British and Dutch ships to capture the Spanish port of Cadiz on the south-west coast of Spain. Arriving there, circumstances made him forego the attempt; but he plundered several smaller, near-by ports, including Port St. Mary, which is important to our story. In this port he found, besides some rich merchandise, plate, jewels, pictures and money, several thousand barrels and casks of *snuff*, manufactured in various parts of Spain. Sir George took the whole lot, snuff included. And it was good snuff of the very finest growth.

With this plunder, the fleet was returning to England

when Sir George, probably still smarting under his Cadiz disappointment, decided to plunder the harbour of Vigo, some 400 miles north of Cadiz with the coast of Portugal filling in the gap. Rooke had learnt, possibly by signal from some other ship—we can think of no other way—that a number of galleons, richly laden, had arrived at Vigo from Havana or thereabouts. So in went Rooke with his fleet, to destroy the greater part of the Spanish shipping. It proved to be Port St. Mary over again.

The plunder was exceedingly valuable and—which concerns us here—included prodigious quantities of snuff from the Havanas, designed for various parts of Spain. Never was seen such a display of bales, bags and scrows. Scrows, by the way, were the untanned skins of buffaloes, sewn into bags, with the raw side outwards, and the hairy side, partly scraped, inwards and in contact with the snuff. Maybe "robustness of character" was one of the qualities claimed for the snuff when ultimately the buffalo skins were well out of sight!

DRAKE'S SHERRY

Still, it was a wonderful haul. Nothing like it had been seen since Drake sailed into Cadiz harbour and got away with 3,000 butts of fine sherry. If butts then were the same as they are today—108 gallons—to be a friend of the bearded buccaneer must have meant something. (At six of our bottles to the gallon, Drake must have swaggered home with close on two million bottles!)

The Port St. Mary and Vigo plunder show to what an enormous extent snuff was used in Spain, probably with France sharing.

The fleet having returned to England, the officers and men set about selling their snuff, of which they had a weight approximating 100 tons. They called it Vigo Snuff or Vigo Prize Snuff, the word "prize" indicating that it had been captured by our ships. This greatly appealed to English admirers of the venturous. There was scarcely a town in England which these excellent snuffs, divorced from their buffalo skins, did not reach. The great impetus given to snuff-taking by these "prizes" established it as firmly in England as it was on the Continent. It has been said that snuff-taking really began on the grand scale in the reign of Queen Anne. One of the reasons for this clearly emerges from the foregoing story; Queen Anne's accession and the Vigo exploits both occurred in 1702.

We have no means of knowing just how the Vigo snuff was treated when it reached this country or to whom the officers and men sold their share. It seems likely that much of it was taken by blenders and ultimately mixed and perfumed so that all tastes were in the end suited.

At this point, snuff's history seems to divide itself, so we will take a couple of pinches ourselves, and start a new chapter on the elegant age of snuff.

CHAPTER II

The Elegant Age

*"Who takes thee not? Where'er I range
I smell they sweets from Pall Mall to the 'Change."*
JAMES BOSWELL, 1740.

BY 1702, when Queen Anne came to the Throne, smoking had had more than a century of supremacy. It had successfully kept snuff largely within the confines of the élite, and, until that year, there was nothing to indicate that things would change very much. Then came the avalanche of Vigo and Port St. Mary snuff described in our last chapter. A writer of the period said there was a positive haze of snuff over Plymouth when Admiral Rooke's ships were unloading, and that "there was much sneezing among the people."

In approaching the second period of snuff's history, we have to view it on two planes—the high and the low, the patrician and the plebeian.

There is not a great deal to be said about the latter. It provided no fabulously elegant snuff-boxes, and inspired no poets, with the possible exception of Rabbie Burns. Snuff did, however, find its way into industries where smoking was forbidden, now that its price was within reach of the workers. Among the trades which took up snuff were printing and tailoring, and snuff-taking still persists in them. Other industries followed suit for no obvious reason except that the workers liked snuff, found it cheaper than tobacco, and easier to use at work. Rapidly the habit spread far and wide.

Obviously the immense stocks of Spanish "prize" snuff could not last indefinitely, although many merchants who bought it from the sailors locked it up and released it piecemeal when they deemed it profitable. Meanwhile it was clear that a new and enormous trade had arisen. Our imports of tobacco leaf grew accordingly, just as snuff-mills were to multiply and increase in size.

The first method of producing snuff in any quantity was by pounding the brittle-dry tobacco leaves in a large pestle-and-mortar. There also came into being small contraptions not unlike coffee-mills, by which the snuff seller in his shop was able to guarantee his snuff to be "specially ground for each customer." He would also no doubt have a large snuff-rasp for the same purpose.

The pocket rasp, or grater, had its vogue at that time, and a great many snuff-takers grated their own snuff from rolls of tobacco called *carottes*, supposedly named, in French, after the shape of that vegetable. These carottes were of well-dried tobacco leaf, tightly rolled after the manner of a cigar. The end of the carotte was rubbed on the rasp in the same way as a nutmeg is grated.

Many of these pocket rasps, which were some four or five inches long, were of great artistic merit, some of them rivalling snuff-boxes in their embellishment. Usually one side was flat and roughed like any grater of today, while the other side was concave, thus forming a cavity into which the grated snuff would fall. At each end of this cavity were receptacles, into which, through apertures, the grated snuff could pass. Generally the rasp would be of tapering shape, so that the receptacle at one end would be larger than that at the other. So, if the snuff-taker wished to fill his snuff-box, he would empty the contents of the larger receptacle into it; but, if he only required a pinch of super-fresh, he shook out a tiny quantity into the smaller receptacle, often shaped as a little shell. This was not large enough to admit the thumb and fingers for a pinch, so the snuff was turned out on the back of the hand, and inhaled from there.

There are still a few of these rasps to be picked up at country sale-rooms, where there may be an argument on "what on earth the thing could have been made for." But it is no use hoping to come across one casually in London, for the antique dealers are usually on to them like hawks as soon as they appear from wherever they have been in hiding over the years.

RASP WITH A HISTORY

A strange example of an elegant snuff-rasp has recently come under our notice. It is credited as having once belonged to Mary Queen of Scots, and is in the possession of a retired clergyman. It is a family heirloom and is supposed to have been given to an ancester named Douglas by Mary herself when rowed across Loch Leven on her escape from Leven Castle in 1568. Snuff had scarcely "got going" in these islands at the time, but it must be remembered that Mary had spent many years in France and had, in fact, married the dauphin Francis in 1558. He succeeded to the throne the next year, but died in the following year. The box may well have been given to her by some French associate during her imprisonment in Leven Castle.

The rasp is part ivory and part silver, with a bust of Queen Mary on the front. The owner's family has always spoken of it as a snuff-box, though it clearly seems to be a rasp, with features that have puzzled the family. "The top part has a small receptacle," writes the owner, "and the front (top?) lifts up disclosing a roughed surface suitable for grating some substance. The top receptacle has a hole in it, and the powder (whatever it was) goes down to the end of the box which has a blunt end." This mystery box was probably of the kind which had space for the carotte when not in use.

These rasps, or graters, went gradually out of fashion when machinery was invented to grind snuff more quickly and efficiently than did the older methods. The rasp in high circles had been an elaborate affair, with several appendages attached by fine gold or silver chains. These would include a small pin for freeing the grater's holes of snuff, a little rake to separate the rough snuff from the smooth, a spoon for transferring snuff from the rasp to the snuff-box, and, rather amusingly, a hare's foot for brushing the snuff from the taker's upper lip!

ROYAL MANIFESTO

It was not surprising, in view of this invasion of snuff-taking, that smoking began to show a decline. In fact, snuff did to smoking what James I was unable to do with his *Counterblaste to Tobacco, a Royal Manifesto* which he issued in 1604; nor yet with his cruel increases in taxation on the herb. His hatred of tobacco in any form was virulent. He increased the 2d. per pound duty on Virginian tobacco to 6s. 10d., while leaving the duty on Spanish tobacco at the original 2d., despite the fact that Virginia had been colonised on our behalf by Sir Walter Raleigh. Possibly the answer to this is that at the time he was hoping to marry the Prince of Wales to the Infanta of Spain.

It is one of the remarkable facts of our history that, however powerful the tryrant, his interference with the simple pleasures of the people usually came to naught. A later example of this was when Charles II issued a Proclamation closing, without further notice, all coffee-houses, of which there were many hundreds in London and the Provinces—each, by the way, with its own large snuff-box, or mull—and each a centre of snuff-takers. But it was neither the coffee nor the snuff which disturbed Charles, but the fact that many of the frequenters of the coffee-houses were too free in their criticisms of the King and Government. " Seminaries of

Sedition " was one term he applied to them. But the majority of the coffee-house fraternity had nothing to do with sedition or anything like it, and at once made a great public outcry. Within ten days this Royal Proclamation was withdrawn, though not without some Royal face-saving strategy which hardly finds place here.

Despite the efforts of James I, smoking held its own for nearly a hundred years, and then Beau Nash did more to undermine it than did either James' diatribe or his cruel impost. Beau Nash is one of those characters more spoken of than known about, and he is sometimes confused with Beau Brummel, although they were not even contemporary. Dandyism, however, they both had in common.

A BRIGHT FELLOW

Beau Nash was the son of a rich glass manufacturer, and, after the usual spells at the university and in the army, he took up law; but he also took up gambling, which proved more rewarding than the stony path of the law. In 1705 he went to live in Bath, which was just entering its period as a fashionable resort. Being the bright fellow which he was, he set about creating attractions, and eventually became the arch-arbiter of the social life of the old and beautiful city— its fashions, amusements and behaviour. He thought smoking in the public rooms and gardens destestable, and because of this he became Snuff's Greatest Friend.

The order went forth from His Elegance, as he was sometimes called, that all smoking in these places should cease. He had no power to do this, yet the result was that Bath's upper crust bowed to him, and before long the other crusts did the same. London Society, which looked to Bath for a lead in many matters, followed suit, and smoking soon gave way to snuff-taking with its elegant rituals. Someone said that to watch a group of Bath dandies taking snuff was like seeing something from a ballet.

London Society dropped their meerschaum pipes with a clatter on their marble floors, and gave their tobacco boxes to their footmen. Women, already snuff-takers and never fond of the smoking habit, took to snuff with increased enthusiasm. The gestures in taking perfumed snuff provided a heaven-sent opportunity to display a pretty hand, an exquisite ring, and even to call attention to a patrician nose.

One reason advanced for women's aversion to smoking was that with their voluminous dresses and monumental hair styles, the smell of tobacco clung perpetually about them. In taking snuff they were but following the example set long ago by Catherine de Medici, as we have read. We shall deal later with further aspects of women and snuff.

The elegant age of snuff had now arrived in full splendour. As an old book, *The Soverane Herbe* puts it: "The beau took it in dainty pinches, his cook in handfuls. Snuff completely displaced smoking in society. To take snuff was an essential part of gallantry. Into the middle of this century (the eighteenth) a snuff-box and a gold-headed cane survived as the professional equipment of a physician. A gentleman who did not take snuff was a contradiction in terms. It is impossible to imagine that age without its constant attendant and master, snuff. Snuff formed as integral a part of the eighteenth century as its be-laced and gallant clothes; its jewelled fingers sought the snuff-box instinctively; to its cynicism, its affectations, its gallantry, its dilettantism, its extravagence and licentiousness, snuff must be added to comprehend it."

It was at about this time that Dr. Johnson said: "Smoking has gone out. To be sure, it is a shocking thing, blowing smoke out of our mouths into other peoples mouths, eyes and noses, and having the same thing done to us."

MR. DRYDEN'S BOX

Reverting to coffee-houses, there still exist, in collections, snuff-boxes which were in use at such famous coffee-houses as Garaway's, Man's, Nando's and a score of others. Among the famous frequenters of these popular places was that "towering" poet, Dryden, whose company was daily sought by the beaux of the time. His favourite house was Will's in Covent Garden, which, in consequence, saw "a parcel of raw, second-rate beaux and wits who were conceited if they had but the honour of dipping a finger and thumb into Mr. Dryden's snuff-box."

To mention Dryden as a snuff-taker is to touch only the fringe of the cavalcade of great men who graced the snuff age, and it is a tribute to " the solace of nose and palate " that they should be remembered for a good couple of centuries as snuff-takers.

Among them were Addison, Steele, Pope, Goldsmith, Dr. Johnson, Garrick and Sir Joshua Reynolds. Indeed, it was said of Reynolds that he took his snuff so carelessly that it often got into his paints, but that his pictures were none the worse for it!

The old *Globe* newspaper once published a slightly satrical, though kindly lampoon of those who dig out the foibles of the great. The occasion was the discovery by a literary researcher that " Keats took Snuff." Thus the *Globe*:

> So " Keats took Snuff " ? A few more years,
> When we are dead and famous—eh ?
> Will they record our pipes and beers,
> And if we smoked cigars or clay ?
> Or will the world cry " Quantum suff "
> To tattle such as " Keats took Snuff " ?
>
> Perhaps some chronicler would wish
> To know what whisky we preferred,
> And if we ever dined on fish,

Or only took the joint and bird.
Such facts are quite as worthy stuff,
Good chronicler, as "Keats took Snuff".

Higher in the scale of snuff-takers we may cite our several Georges. One of these, the most inveterate of them all, was George IV, who treated snuff with the greatest veneration. It is said of him that, when taking a pinch at a masked ball, a gallant, perhaps not recognising him, took a pinch from the royal box. This was too much for George. To have a stranger's thumb and forefinger in contact with his snuff was unthinkable. He flung the box away; nor did he trouble to retrieve it. George's mother, Queen Charlotte, and his wife Caroline, were also great snuff-takers, as were other ladies of the times, and we shall meet them in our later chapter on snuff-taking ladies.

It was not our intention, in speaking of famous snuff-takers, to stray far from " our right little, tight little island," as it was once called; but there we are ! Who could resist a few words about the Little Corporal, *le petit homme gris*—the little grey man—as the poilus of his day called him—the Emperor Napoleon ?

SECRET LOYALTY

Napoleon was indeed a great snuff-taker, but accounts differ as to his methods of taking it. Some say he carried leather-lined waistcoat pockets, as Dr. Samuel Johnson did, and took hearty pinches when the stress of a campaign mounted to a climax. On the other hand, we have the account of Constant, the French writer. " It has been asserted," he says, " that his Majesty took an inordinate deal of snuff; and that in order to take it with greater facility, he carried it in his waistcoat pockets. This is altogether untrue; he never took it except from a snuff-box; and, though he used a great deal, he took but little. He would frequently hold

A sniff for each nostril.   Old bone snuff-taking spoon

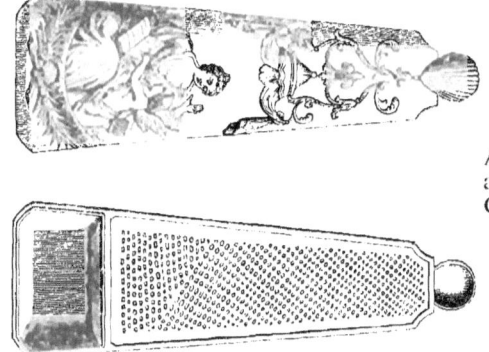

Antique Snuff-rasp (back and front) described in Chapter II

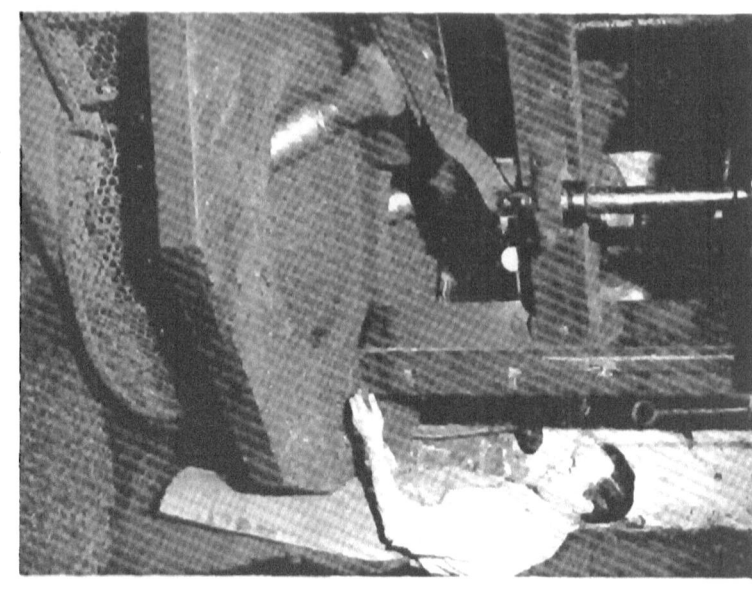

Mechanical snuff-grinding pestle and mortar

Ancient water-wheel driving snuff-making machinery at Kendal

the snuff-box to his nose merely to smell it; at other times he would take a pinch from the box, smell it and throw it away. Thus it would happen that the spot where he was sitting or standing would be strewed with snuff."

An interesting story comes of this. During his exile in the isle of Elba his supporters in France—and they were many—used snuff perfumed with essential oil of violet, violet being the favourite perfume of the Emperor, whether in his snuff or not we do not know. There was a secret code among his supporters. Offering a pinch (perhaps from a box shaped like Napoleon's hat) they would ask pointedly, "Do you like this perfume?" Whereupon the other Bonapartist would reply: " I long for the spring, when the flower now faded shall again wear the purple, and when its breath shall be felt even farther than its colour can be seen." A pretty touch of secret loyalty ! Sure enough, the flower bloomed again, but it was due to fade finally at St. Helena.

This chapter, whether we like it or not, must conclude with a few notes on the eventual decline of snuff-taking. It had reached such social heights that a backward slide was almost inevitable. As the great physicist and philosopher, Sir Isaac Newton, had propounded long before: every action is accompanied by an equal and opposite reaction. Snuff had gone up like a rocket and, although it did not exactly come down like the stick, it sustained a severe bump.

The reasons were several. One of them was the changing world. In the upper realms of society snuff-taking and its rituals had come to verge on the ridiculous, and ridicule is often deadly. As the age of foppery declined, so did snuff, for in foppery had lain much of its popularity.

CIGAR DIVANS

But there were more concrete reasons to come. There was the appearance of choice cigars at reasonable prices, and the opening of countless " cigar divans ", where men might sit in company, call for refreshment, and read the daily newspapers provided as part of the service. Then came a further blow—the introduction of the lazy man's smoke, the cigarette, which vastly increased in favour when it was sent out in great quantities to our soldiers in the Crimea. Snuff-taking, in boxing parlance, was showing signs of distress, but the knock-out did not come.

The impression that snuff died out is entirely fallacious; otherwise why should the centuries-old snuff-mills in Kendal and Sheffield have continued to prosper to this day, and why did Smith's Snuff Shop live on, comparatively unperturbed? The snuff slump, if such it were, affected mainly the great range of foreign and fancy snuffs which had been pouring into England for so long. And so, when we speak of snuff's present-day rise to favour, it must not be imagined that the rise is from zero.

Far, far from it.

CHAPTER III

Snuff in the Making

"*For every pinch of snuff we take
Helps trade in some degree.*"
READ'S WEEKLY JOURNAL, 1762.

IT is a long way from the broad, coarse tobacco leaf which has been brought to our docks to the elegant, silky powder in our snuff-box. There have been many processes at work. Firstly, the leaves have been put into Government bond, there to await the snuff-maker with his cheque to pay the exorbitant demands of the Customs before he may remove this simple commodity to his own care and his own snuff-mill. This accomplished, the owner of the leaves sets out to convert them into snuff. It isn't quite so easy as that, of course, as we shall presently see.

It is a mistake, by the way, to suppose that all the well-known snuffs produced by the mills are entirely their own prerogative. As Mr. Hugh McCausland, the eminent authority on snuff, succinctly pointed out: "Additions are ever being made to a long list of proprietary prepared brands and blends. Distinct types of snuff, on the other hand, remain limited to those bearing such widely known names as S.P., Kendal Brown and High Toast. These are general descriptions of snuff types rather than names; they indicate types which are ground by a number of manufacturers and are not the prerogative of particular firms. The three mentioned are among the oldest, as they are certainly the most in demand, of the snuffs of Britain and Ireland."

That High Toast in its various forms is Ireland's favourite will surprise no one who reads the amusing account of its inception in our last chapter—"Snuff in Story and Song."

Within the snuff types mentioned above, you may find certain variations. Thus, the Kendal Brown you obtain from Smith's may be made to a specification of that firm, based on customers' inclinations and arrived at by experiments, then to be followed by the manufacturing mills.

In England, snuff is made chiefly in the two towns of Sheffield and Kendal, the first being in the heart of industrial Yorkshire, and the other in the beautiful Lakeland county of Westmorland. Until a few years ago a sizeable amount of snuff was made in the little market town of Devizes in Wiltshire, but this is so no longer. Nor is it now made at Mitcham in Surrey, though at one time it made most of the English snuff used in London. It stands on the little river Wandle, whose waters originally worked the Mitcham snuff-mills. But snuff-making there died out, giving way to the lavender-growing industry which, alas, has also practically gone.

WATER MILLS

The basic method of making snuff has not changed greatly by age or locality, except that modern machinery has, of course, appeared at the expense of the more romantic water-mills, many of which had previously operated in the grinding of flour. Thus, snuff-grinding at Sheffield and Kendal began with the water-wheel. The old-time mill machinery is by no means obsolete, as is evinced by some of it having been incorporated with the now prevalent power-driven machinery, as at both Sheffield and Kendal.

The basic method referred to is roughly this: " The stalks and leaf may be taken from tobacco grown in any of the tobacco growing countries, and ground into snuff, the stalk (or centre part of the leaf), being used mainly for the coaser-grained snuffs. In addition, snuff sometimes contains what are known in the trade as 'Shorts and Smalls,' i.e., broken leaf and small pieces of tobacco which cannot, on account of size, be used in the ordinary processes of cigarette and pipe-tobacco making.

"The blend of these materials will depend on the colour and flavour of the particular snuff it is intended to manufacture. After that, art, inspiration, inventiveness and a good nose come into the picture. The whole thing is a highly specialised business in which secret methods and recipes, handed down from generation to generation, and the blending of raw material to obtain the right texture, flavour and aroma are work for which a natural aptitude and years of experience are required."

In the case of one firm, the recipe for its principal snuff is carried only in the heads of its two chief proprietors, though a written copy of it is lodged with the bank.

"It will suffice to say that the blended material is ground to a powder in a number of different processes. Old-fashioned mills with oak mortars and iron pestles are used (at Kendal) for the coarser snuffs; but the dry, finely-powdered varieties are ground in modern disintegrating machines. During these processes certain salts are added, and the finished snuff is a scented one, or a blend of different scents. In the flavourings, only essential oils are permitted. It should be mentioned that there is strict supervision over the manufacture of snuff, and any manufacturer found by the Government Analyst to be using a prohibited substance would be subject to heavy penalties."

FERMENTATION

Before the pulverising stage, the leaves receive much scientific attention. Sometimes they are damped and allowed to reach the point of fermentation. But such treatments, as with recipes and added perfumes, are often family secrets.

The word "family" is used advisedly, for the chief snuff firms are family concerns, and have been so for generations.

Snuff was first manufactured in Kendal in about 1740 by one, Matthew Whittaker, but there are no records to say what happened to his venture. However, in 1792 a Thomas Harrison went to Scotland, and came back to Kendal with an idea, a formula, some second-hand snuff-milling machinery *and* a burning belief that he could produce the finest snuffs in the country.

On the death of Thomas Harrison, his son-in-law, Samuel Gawith, took over. Since then there have always been Gawiths in the Kendal snuff industry. In 1867, a John Illingworth, one of Gawith's commercial travellers, started making snuff on his own account, and the name Illingworth has long appeared in the annals of Kendal snuff-making. It is interesting to note that John Illingworth and a Henry Hoggarth were trustees of Samuel Gawith's will, and that a Hoggarth and a succeeding Gawith joined forces in the snuff business. Hence the present firm's name of Gawith Hoggarth and Co., Ltd.

Kendal lies in a Westmorland valley and, if viewed from one of the neighbouring fells, presents but a minority of red roofs. Nearly all the buildings are roofed with greenish-grey Westmorland slate. The local accent is like that of Lancashire, yet unlike it. "There's nowt like Kendal" has long been the natives' dictum when it comes to keeping a boastful visitor in his place.

On a dominating hill stand the ruins of Kendal Castle, home of Katherine Parr, the lady whom Henry VIII married, and who managed to outlive him. The town is small as towns go—about 17,000—and is some seven miles from the lapping shores of Lake Windermere. A pleasant home town for the "fragrant pinch!"

Another family name in the snuff world is that of Wilson's of Sheffield. Although Sheffield may lack the rural amenities of Kendal, it has the compensation of being the home of that well-known snuff—S.P. Various reasons for thus naming the snuff have been adduced. Some devotees like to think the initials stand for " Sheffield Pride," though the likeliest explanation is that they stand for " Sp," an abbreviation of the word Spanish applied to the snuff in its earlier days.

Actually, there are two firms by name of Wilson in the City of Steel, and both are of the same family. They are J. & H. Wilson, Ltd., and Wilson's & Co. (Sharrow), Ltd. They are friendly rivals. They began as a single Wilson in 1746. He was Joseph Wilson who was making snuff in a little mill on a stream called the Porter. He prospered and, in about a hundred years' time the firm became top-heavy with Wilsons, so to speak, and two of them started in partnership at Westbrook Mill, as distinct from Sharrow Mill, where they had been in partnership with their cousins, William and George.

We feel we should apologise for omitting such other towns as make snuffs of quality, but, in a short book of this kind, so it must be!

CHAPTER IV

A Guide to Snuff Varieties

"*When other snuffs are offered me,
I cling to my old friend Rappee.
Though each is called the King of Snuff,
For me Black Rappee is enough.*"
PARSON MELLOR, 1790.

THE varieties of snuff, as Sam Weller's father might have said, are extensive and peculiar. They range from the early *Bergamottes* to the modern *Town Clerk*; from the *Rappees* of the Georges to the *Cardinals* of today. Present-day varieties, though numerous, are far fewer than those when Britain was importing snuff from widely scattered parts of the world. The origin of many of the latter may be guessed from their names, of which a few are Cuba, Romano's Hollande, Best Brazil, Light Dutch, Dunkerque Rappee, Copenhagen, Violet Strasburg and a host of others. After a time, with the growth of English and Scottish snuff-mills, foreign snuffs became but a memory—a memory kept alive by various makers reproducing to some extent the qualities and flavours of the past.

A real "stand-by" snuff of the early periods was Rappee, its name deriving from the French word *raper*, to grate or to rasp. It was usually a rather coarse snuff, often flavoured with Attar of Roses, "the most costly perfume ever known to man." Many millions of rose petals are needed to make one pound of Attar at a cost of £25 per ounce. Snuff so flavoured was the favourite of the Prince

Regent (later George IV), and Prince's Mixture, as it was often called, remains a popular snuff today, under that same name.

Fairholt, in his valuable book on tobacco, written a hundred years ago, says: " Rappee may be considered as the parent of all other snuffs." An older writer goes further. " Good, wholesome rappee, whether brown or black, coarse of fine, is the proper snuff for a continuance. It is the snuff of the business man, of litterati, of professionals, of all, in fact, who take snuff for its utility in sharpening the wits, in stimulating the brain . . . Rappee is the perfect manly snuff."

Black Rappee still holds a place among the snuffs obtainable at Smith's Snuff Shop, but, so many snuffs having been devised since the above eulogy was written, it hardly comes first in the list today.

The selection of snuffs, all individually described, in the latter part of this chapter, shows what a wide variety is at the choice of the snuff-taker today. It details the different fragrant tobacco leaves which come to us from far-away places to be converted into basic snuffs which, in turn, are treated with appropriate essential oils and essences. The nature and proportions of these, as we have remarked elsewhere, are jealously guarded by the possessors of the individual " recipes," many of which have been family secrets for a century or two.

GUARDED SECRECY

The guarded secrecy which surrounds the perfuming of snuff has a happy parallel in the famous Chartreuse liqueurs, green and yellow. The flavours of these potent delights have baffled would-be imitators for centuries, and they are still a well-kept secret of the monks who created them. It has been said that the distillation of 130 herbs are introduced into the basis of a special cognac brandy.

To digress a little, we may mention that the history of

the Chartreux Fathers reveals an undue proportion of misfortunes. The latest of these was in 1903 when the monks were expelled from their monastery by French law. They took refuge in Spain, where they resumed making their liqueurs in the old style. Meanwhile, the French Government seized the famous brand of liqueur, and soon it was being produced on a commercial scale.

At least, so it was fondly hoped by the usurpers; but they had overlooked the fact that the monks, conscious to the last, had taken their true recipe with them. Every effort was made to imitate the product, but those in the neighbourhood who had known the real thing laughed openly at the self-conscious " manufacturers " when they met them in the streets.

Thirty-seven years later, the monks were back in their monastery, La Grande Chartreuse, and things went on placidly as before; which seems to show you can't keep a good monk down.

Among the snuffs listed ahead is one called *Tonquin,* which presents a minor paradox to the uninitiated, inasmuch as it is one of the least called-for snuffs yet with a name known among snuff-takers far and wide. It contains ground-up Tonquin beans which grow on the tonquin tree, a native of Venezuela. This is an evergreen tree 60 feet high, bearing clustered spikes of violet-coloured flowers. These flowers are succeeded by short pods each containing a single fragrant bean, known as the Tonquin (or Tonka) bean which, apart for its use as snuff, is in considerable demand for scenting sachet powders.

TONQUIN BEANS

And the paradox? Great numbers of snuff-takers the world over keep a Tonquin bean in their snuff-box, to add its perfume to that already there. Most snuff-takers, however, are content to be loyal to the flavour of their own chosen snuff. Just when the Tonquin bean custom began is difficult to ascertain, but it is believed to have started in far-off days in Venezuela where the Tonquin tree grows.

One must surely wonder how Jockey Club (another listed snuff) came by its name. At first guess we would say it is flavoured with some of the ingredients which went into the old-time Jockey Club scent, so beloved of our grandmothers when they were girls. And perhaps it is. But how came the scent itself to be so named? There is nothing very sentimental about the Jockey Club as we know it, since it is a body (founded 1750) which governs trainers and jockeys with an iron hand. Mr. Aytoun Ellis, in his fascinating book on perfumes, *Essence of Beauty* (1960), tells us that the scent was originally "a bouquet compounded of bergamot, jasmine, mimosa, tuberose, orris and violet in imitation of the pleasant fragrance that pervaded the Downs at Epsom in the late spring, and was wafted across the course from the woods to the Jockey Club in the Grandstand." With all respect to our friend Mr. Ellis we suggest that this story be taken with a pinch of snuff.

We also learn from the same author that Bergamot (mentioned elsewhere in these pages) is an essential oil expressed from the fresh peel of *Citrus Bergamia,* which grows exclusively in the southern part of the Italian province of Reggio-Calabria, and that the oil has a prominent place in the formulae of both eau-de-Cologne and lavender water.

The most expensive snuff to be bought today is Café Royale, which is 15s. per ounce, as against others varying from 4s. 6d. to 13s. 5d. Perhaps, when he has read a little further, the reader may begin to understand why this is so. (His understanding will be completed when he tries Café Royale!) It is a dark snuff whose flavour was inspired by the aroma of coffee, brandy and cream, perhaps at the end of a good dinner. Be that as it may, the blenders got to work and produced the present snuff. It is a fine blend of North

American and Oriential tobaccos, the leaves being specially treated beforehand to release the natural aroma. After making, it is perfumed with pure essential oil of coffee, backed by certain rarely found spices. To ensure perfection when it reaches the customer, it is kept for a year in sealed bottles, to make certain that not even a hint of its flavour shall have escaped. Café Royale owes its inception entirely to Smith's of Charing Cross Road.

The name Town Clerk does not sound romantic, yet this elegant snuff is not without its story. A genial gentleman, a customer of Smith's, was in the habit of asking for a mixture of several snuffs which he specified. So that he should not have to wait at the counter while the snuff was blended, the firm always had a bottle of it ready for whenever he should call. So far it had no name. Quite unexpectedly, Smith's learnt that their connoisseur customer was the Town Clerk of an important borough. After that, it was no longer a nameless snuff!

Another snuff with an unexpected history is called George IV. Both as Prince Regent and King, this monarch was, as described earlier, a snuff-taker of amazing capacity. Yet the snuff was not deliberately named after him.

At the time of the coronation of a later George, Smith's window exhibited a framed picture of the so-called "first gentleman in Europe." On the shelf, leaning against the picture, was a card bearing the name George IV. As it happened, the card fell off the shelf, to land upright in a bowl of snuff below. No one in the shop was aware of this until a customer entered and asked for "an ounce of George IV."

Thus another snuff acquired its name.

We may now turn to our short review of the many happily-named snuffs whose fragrance gives charm to the old shop in the Charing Cross Road; in other words, to our Guide to Snuff Varieties.

GOLDEN CARDINAL. This fine mild snuff is manufactured from specially selected leaves of North American and Oriental tobaccos carefully blended to maintain texture, pungency and colour. The perfume of fine aromatic herbs and Oriental spices is selected with the greatest care from each year's crop to give overall continuity to the final blend.

ROYAL CARDINAL. A blend of North American and Oriental tobaccos. It is perfumed with the purest Tonquin essence with an underlying "nose" of pure flower essences.

ORANGE CARDINAL. Is manufactured from specially selected leaves of North American and Oriental tobaccos, double sieved to ensure perfect mixing. More than fifty different perfumes, laboratory blended and balanced, give this snuff its rich, distinctive "nose".

ENGLISH CARDINAL. A high-dried snuff flavoured with a special compound of essential oils having a predominately lemon flavour.

RED CARDINAL. A rich, full blend of North American, African and Oriental tobaccos perfumed with a delicately balanced blend of pure flower extracts.

WHITE CARDINAL. A choice blend of Commonwealth tobaccos, lightly flavoured with menthol and a background of finest Mediterranean fruit essences and English flower essences. Recommended for relief from catarrh.

APPLE BLOSSOM. This is a snuff of the light dry variety with a distinctive Apple perfume.

ATTAR OF ROSES. A full-bodied but mild snuff delightfully flavoured with Bulgarian Attar of Roses. A perfect after-dinner snuff.

BLACK RAPPEE. A coarse-milled moist unflavoured snuff prepared from well-fermented fire-cured Nyasaland Puducah tobacco.

CAFE ROYALE. Specially manufactured from a blend of North American and Oriental tobaccos, specially treated before grinding to release its natural aroma. It is perfumed with a pure coffee essence backed up with a "nose" of many fine spices.

CARNATION No. 41. A blend of the finest selected North American and Oriental tobaccos, specially treated to increase the natural pungency in order that it may carry the highly concentrated perfume of Carnation extract. This is backed up with a sutble " nose " of other flower concentrates.

CONSORT. A rich dark snuff fairly coarse milled and slightly scented.

COPENHAGEN (Chewing). A chewing snuff, roughly-ground from well-fermented fire-cured Nyasaland and Tanganyika leaf. Natural flavour.

CUBA. A very mild, well-balanced blend of West Indian tobaccos. This snuff is virtually unflavoured, but has just a suspicion of Oriental oils to bring out the " nose ".

GARDEN MINT. A blend of North American and Oriental tobaccos. It is perfumed with a mixture of the finest mint oils blended with other background oils and essences.

GEORGE IV. A fine-milled snuff having a refreshing spicy flavour. Careful sieving ensures the silky texture of this snuff.

GOLDEN LAVENDER. A mild delicate snuff slightly perfumed with pure Lavender.

GRAND OPERA. A rather pungent snuff with a rich spicy flavour.

HELIOTROPE. A special blend of North American and Oriental tobaccos which carries to best advantage the delicate Heliotrope perfume.

IRISH HIGH TOAST. The lightest and driest snuff on the market. This is a strong snuff with a toasted flavour. This snuff is not for the beginner.

JOCKEY CLUB. A light dry snuff highly scented with Jockey Club perfume in its purest form.

KENDAL BROWN. A coarse-milled moist snuff blended and flavoured to the original 1791 recipe.

LATAKIA. A pungent natural flavoured snuff made from the finest Syrian mountain-type leaf.

LAVENDER. A light fine snuff heavily perfumed with oil of Lavender.

LEMON. Is manufactured from North American and Oriental tobaccos, and perfumed with a balanced blend of citrous oils.

MENTHOL EXTRA. A medium-strength Menthol snuff.

OTTERBURN. A mild highly-perfumed snuff of distinct characteristics blended from Kentucky Burley and West Indian air-cured tobacco. Extra fine milled.

PEPPERMINT. A light pungent snuff flavoured with oil of Peppermint.

PRINCES DARK. One of the oldest snuffs dating back to Regency days. A flavoured, moist dark, almost black snuff. Coarse-milled.

ROSE. A finely ground snuff delicately flavoured with Attar of Roses.

SPANISH. A pungent unscented snuff specially prepared for the connoisseur.

SPECIAL "M". A pungent medium ground snuff with almond flavour.

SUPERB. A rather milder snuff with almond flavour backed with other fine spices.

SUPER MENTHOL. A strong sharp mentholated snuff.

S.P. BEST. A pungent unflavoured snuff carefully fine-milled and sieved to ensure perfect even texture.

TONQUIN. A light dry snuff flavoured with oil of tonquin.

TOWN CLERK. A subtle blend of floral and aromatic oils.

VIOLET. A blend of Commonwealth tobaccos. The perfume is predominantly pure extract of Violet, but this is cleverly balanced with a selection of the finest quality fixatives.

WALLFLOWER. A fine-ground snuff delicately perfumed with essence of Wallflower.

No. 30 SPECIAL. A fine milled snuff slightly spiced.

No. 74 SPECIAL. A strong pungent snuff with just a trace of spices added.

CHAPTER V

Snuff-taking Today

Let others toil for wealth or fame,
To get a fortune or a name,
  Of these I've got enough;
For other gifts, old friend, I'll pray,
Grant me, unto my latest day,
  Grant me a pinch of snuff!
ANON. 1850.

SOME industries, more than others, use snuff as a matter of course. Among them are printing and tailoring, whose workers have taken snuff almost since it was introduced. It has lately been reported from the northern counties that miners are buying snuff in increased quantities, perhaps as a newly-found reaction to the age-old ban on smoking in the pits. The same may be said of factory workers, male and female, whose employers discountenance smoking, perhaps because it is a waste of time which, by comparison, snuff is not. Further, smoking is something of a soporific, whereas snuff is a mental stimulent, a fact of which employers are no doubt aware.

Recently the Royal Air Force has taken to snuff in a big way, to provide momentary relaxation and diversion when flying, during which smoking is generally forbidden. Motorists are also taking to snuff in increasing numbers, especially those making long journeys, such as lorry-drivers, for it has a keep-you-awake property not found in smoking. The banning of smoking in many theatres is also responsible for much snuff-taking. And so we might go on. One man of our acquaintance even carries snuff in addition to ordinary

A selective customer tries out a snuff

Top: Two modern silver snuff-boxes. *Below:* Gold and jewelled box given by Elizabeth I to King Philip of Spain

smoking materials in case, during the rush hours in city trains, he finds himself forced either to let his train go without him or bundle himself into a non-smoking compartment.

It is good to think that a few of the pleasant customs attached to snuff in its Regency hey-day still adhere to it. One exception is the ritual of taking a pinch, which periodically brought down on itself a measure of ridicule, as well it might. We refer to this elsewhere; meanwhile here is an amusing little lampoon of a certain type of snuff-taker in those days:

"There is a species of long-armed snuff-taker, that performs the operation in a style of potent and elaborate preparation. He first puts his head on one side, then stretches forth his arm with a pinch in his hand, then brings round his hand as a snuff-taking elephant might with his trunk; and finally shakes snuff, head and nose together, in a sudden vehemence of convulsion."

It was Addison, if memory serves, who said: "Let me see a man take a pinch of snuff, and I will tell you what he is." Apparently our psychologists have not yet thought of that one!

"PINS' POINTS"

Leigh Hunt had something to say about snuff-takers who "get the thing over as quickly as possible." He called them epigrammatic snuff-takers, who come to the point as fast as possible, and to whom pungency is everything. They generally use a sharp snuff—a sort of *essence of pins' points."* (This is good!) "Whenever you meet with a man such as this, you need never be deceived. If your interview be on a matter of business, never attempt to beat about the bush—never have recourse to anything like chincanery. Rely on it, that such a snuff-taker is a thorough business man, and will not be imposed upon. He will go straight to the business in hand, and will knock it off with as much rapidity as he takes his pinch of snuff."

One of the happy customs which still prevail concerns the appearance of the large snuff-box, or mull, on the tables of regimental messes. As *Punch* recently said: " . . . young officers feel they would be lacking in respect for the heroes of Blenheim and Badajoz if they did not help themselves to the contents of those splendid silver-capped ramshorns, with spoon, rake and brush attached."

In some cases, regimental and others, the snuff is taken while the port is going round, which is a practice originated by George IV. This can hardly be to the liking of those eminent wine connoisseurs of today—for ever in and out of print—who, by a sniff of a wine's bouquet, will tell you its year, the commune from whence it came, and perhaps the colour of the vineyard owner's hair!

The snuff-mull, about which we speak in the chapter on snuff-boxes, is widely used at functions today. Thus, many out-lying clubs possess one of these capacious boxes, and take it with them on such occasions as a dinner in Town. One in particular we know. It is at Dulwich, and always takes its snuff-box to the Café Royal in London on the occasion of its annual dinner. (We wonder if they fill it with Smith's super-choice snuff, Café Royale, whose name, by the way, has a French origin and has nothing to do with the famous café in Regent Street.)

SIR WINSTON'S BOX

Quite the most famous "communal" snuff-box is that in the House of Commons. Not only has it been used regularly by Sir Winston Churchill, but was actually presented by him to Mr. W. A. Brimson, the Chief Doorkeeper. It had long been the custom for the Chief Doorkeeper to be in charge of a substantial snuff-box, which he kept filled at the Government's expense. (Literally "on the House!") Members would take a pinch on their way in or out of the Chamber, among them the Prime Minister, Mr. Churchill, himself. Then came the Blitz when, among other things blown out of sight, was the Chief Doorkeeper's snuff-box. This was in October, 1941. When Sir Winston heard of it he showed great concern. " We will have another one," he said, and without delay presented a fine Georgian snuff-box to the Chief Doorkeeper. As there are about a hundred snuff-takers in the House of Commons today, Sir Winston's box does not lack patronage.

Another " communal " snuff-box resides at the Mansion House, and is the property of the Corporation of London. It is a fine box, but has not been out for an airing for many a long day. The last Lord Mayor to have it on view—and on tap—was Sir Leslie Boyce, who was First Citizen in 1951. Who knows but a near-future Mayoral election may not bring forth another snuff-taker ?

One might not imagine snuff to be associated with first-class cricket, yet there is in Lord's Pavilion today a snuff-box which calls up great memories of the game. It is a strange box, of silver, and shaped like a coffin, a shape explained by its having been the property of W. G. Grace's brother, who was a coroner, a point not overlooked by one, T. C. O'Brien, who presented it to him ! The inscription on the box, apart from a cryptic Latin quotation, is: " From T.C.O'B. to E.M.G., Clifton, August 1894." Just how the box passed from E. M. Grace, W.G.'s brother, to Lord's is not easy to discover, though perhaps easier to guess.

There is also at Lord's a large mother-of-pearl and silver-gilt snuff-box used by members of the M.C.C. in the Clubroom during the proprietorship of J. H. Dark, 1835—1864.

ST. CLEMENT DANES

The use of snuff boxes as presentations goes back far in the history of snuff. One of the earliest we have found is on view in a glass case in the church of St. Clement Danes, islanded in the Strand near the Law Courts. It was presented by a patron to the Churchwardens as early as 1686. Another snuff-box, placed beside it is of the more recent nineteenth century. St. Clement Danes is the church referred to in the much-loved nursery rhyme, "Oranges and Lemons." Alas, it was gutted by two air raids, and the bells, which once pealed out the tune of Oranges and Lemons, were destroyed. The church, however, was rebuilt and, happily, the new bells still ring out the old tune. The church has been "made over" to the Royal Air Force, and has now become their own church, many R.A.F. services being held there. An interesting feature is the marble floor of the nave in which are inset the crests, in slate, of around three hundred R.A.F. Squadrons, each separate.

We have referred to regimental snuff-boxes, but it is fitting in this respect to refer to the Royal Fusiliers (City of London Regiment) which has its headquarters in Finsbury Square. This regiment possesses four snuff-boxes, two of which repose in the Tower of London, with which the regiment is connected.

The clergy, as we are aware, were always "ones for snuff," and a tradition of snuff-taking still seems to lurk in the neighbourhood of St. Paul's Cathedral. We do not know if Sir Christopher Wren took snuff, though he finished his days in the very height of the snuff age. We do know, however, that many eminent clerics of the Cathedral took their snuff, including that very witty minor canon, Henry Barham, famous for all time through his Ingoldsby Legends, one of which tells the story of "The Jackdaw of Rheims." So today we must not be surprised to be offered a pinch when one meets "the Cathedral men" round about the top of Ludgate Hill.

We do not know if they use any particular brand of snuff, but it would not be unfitting for S.P. to be a favourite around St. Paul's!

CHAPTER VI

The Lure of the Snuff-box

"*What strange and wondrous virtue must there be
And secret charm, O Snuff, concealed in thee!
That bounteous Nature and inventive Art,
Bedecking thee, thus all their powers exert.*"
ARBUCKLE, 1719.

THE snuff-box in its day has occupied a position in our national life held by no other personal object. This applies particularly to its ubiquity in the Regency period and the half-century which followed it. Those were the days when snuff-boxes were of great account to one and all, from servants to sovereigns. Thus, Daniel ("Robinson Crusoe") Defoe was wont to declare that his servant-girl took her snuff with the air of a duchess, while George ("First Gentleman in Europe") IV complained that many of his courtiers took their snuff with a lack of the elegant touch.

Further, as an old journal has it: "No other object of *vertu* has been more patronised by the crowned heads of Europe—(and there were once quite a lot of them)—for purposes of presentation, diplomatic and otherwise, than the snuff-box." As evidence of its importance in keeping up relations with foreign powers, we need only quote from the account of sums expended at the coronation of the said Gentleman George:

> Messrs. Randell and Bridge for snuff-boxes to Foreign Ministers: £8,205 15s. 5d.

This amounts to about £40,000 of our present money.

If nothing else gives authenticity to this fantastic figure, surely the five-pence does.

Most of these boxes would be of gold, inset with various jewelled designs; or perhaps they bore the Royal cipher in diamonds. Where are they now? we might wonder. Perhaps we should look for them in museums maintained by some monarchy-denuded capitals of Europe, or in small, selective museums such as the *Musée d'interê national du Tabac* at Bergerac (Dordogne) which today presents a charming exhibition of snuff-boxes. Or, perhaps, we might find them among the hereditary treasures of some ancient families over whom the wars have passed. Be sure of this, however, they are not being overlooked.

Some of them will have found their way into collections in this country or America, *via* such doyens of art auctioneers as Christie's and Sotheby's. As mentioned elsewhere, a snuff-box was sold in March, 1962, by the latter firm for 2,000 guineas. It was what is today called an "Automation Snuff-box" in gold and enamel, the lid decorated with a picture of children playing by a lake, flanked by miniatures of classical statues in alcoves. One of these alcoves, when opened, discloses a watch, while another reveals a country scene with a windmill in working order.

Of course, snuff-boxes like this rarely come into the market, but Sotheby's records tell us of many less ingenious specimens fetching prices nearly as high.

Apart from the intrinsic and artistic value of old snuff-boxes, they have yet another claim upon us—by virtue of the intimacy of their history. It is difficult to handle a Regency box, of whatever value, without enjoying the memories it conjures up. In its time it may have fitted snugly into the pockets of a score of brocaded waistcoats, its lid lifted by the fingers of a dozen elegant owners, its contents offered delicately to a hundred-and-one fellow snuff-takers. It may have been handed round when the battle of Blenheim was celebrated, and when Trafalgar was the day's fresh news. Incidently, the writer has a plain brass, oval snuff-box, bevelled and lead-lined, on which is inscribed in scrolled, long-S lettering: *Thomas Wilson,* 1805. The date, of course, is that of Trafalgar. Who was Thomas Wilson, and how came he to have his box engraved in that year? It is pleasant to wonder.

YEARS OF CONFLICT

As snuff and snuff-boxes were in such universal use during the eighteenth century, it is worth taking a look at that remarkable period. It may help us to understand some of the foibles of those days. It was a strange period and bred a strange kind of Englishman. The reason is not far to seek, for, excepting a few peaceful gaps, that century saw us almost perpetually at war with one country or another, sometimes in a life-or-death struggle. Among these conflicts was the War of the Spanish Succession, with its famous battles of Blenheim and Ramillies. This war over, it was not long before we were again at war with Spain and then, almost simultaneously, with France. Soon after these were sorted out we had the Seven Years' War against France, with Prussia on our side. This ended with the Treaty of Paris. We also had the War of American Independence, and such " irritants " as the Jacobite Rebellions and their ultimate battles, and Clive's campaigns in India. Finally, after the French Revolution, we had the French *Republic* at our throats, with Napoleon and his snuff-boxes in the lead. For a time we stood alone against France and other countries of the Continent, much as we did against Hitler in the last war. It was tough going. But in the year of Thomas Wilson's brass snuff-box, Trafalgar (followed later by Waterloo) heralded an era of peace. But we were out of the eighteenth century by then.

There appears a slight link between Horatio Nelson and Thomas Wilson with his 1805 box. Each was a snuff-taker, and Nelson's snuff-box survives in the Naval Museum at Greenwich. Thomas Wilson's is still in the obscurity of the writer's possession !

It has been maintained that this period of incessant war greatly affected English life, which is quite probable. As one writer put it: " In that age of beaux, snuff reigned paramount. It was carried to an excess characteristic of the period. Only natural, indeed, were these excesses. It was an age of extremes, of struggles with primal elements. The life-or-death struggles that England was engaged in reflected itself in the foppery and the poverty; the stark atheism, with hard drinking, high gambling and fashionable viciousness of the century."

We have digressed a little, but, as the eighteenth century and snuff-boxes were so interwoven, it was perhaps as well to take a look behind the scenes.

IT RAINED SNUFF-BOXES

The use of snuff-boxes as presentations did not end at coronations. The presentation of a snuff-box as a mark of esteem was very general, and Horace Walpole—letter writer, intellectual and gossip-spreader—said of Pitt that upon his retirement from statesmanship, " it rained snuff-boxes upon him for a month."

There seemed no materials pleasing to the eye which were not used in the making of snuff-boxes. Among them, apart from enamelled gold and silver, were glass, porcelain, amber, jade, ivory, tortoise-shell, brass, agate, wood, horn, papier-mâché and pewter. The last one had a great vogue, and still has, pewter snuff-boxes being made today in numbers which increase as snuff-taking climbs again up the social ladder.

Pewter is a metal alloy of great charm and long history. The London city livery company, the Pewterers' Company, which formerly had considerable powers over the making of pewter, dates back to the fourteenth century. Its first livery hall, built 200 years earlier, was destroyed in the Great Fire of London. It was rebuilt, burnt down again in 1840, and once more rebuilt. Today, in E.C.2, this later hall still stands.

Pewter, ordinarily speaking, consists of 80 per cent. tin and 20 per cent. lead. There are other pewters, one of them consisting of antimony, bismuth and copper, with no lead at all. This is known as plate pewter, and has its own specific uses. Old pewter, as exemplified in bygone drinking vessels, is much sought after by collectors.

As mentioned earlier, Smith's offer an interesting selection of pewter snuff-boxes, many of them being embossed with sporting scenes. It is a matter of note that these designs are stamped with the original dies once used in the decoration of powder-flasks before the introduction of sporting cartridges, and when the old muzzle-loading guns were in use.

Papier-mâché, as its name implies, is made of pulped paper mixed with other materials. It is rarely used in making boxes today. At one time it was common to introduce potato-skin into the mixture, as it had the property of keeping snuff at a proper temperature. For, let it be said, the old snuff-takers were as particular about the temperature of their snuff as they were about that of their wine. Snuff is a sensitive creature. It will exude or withhold its bouquet according to the insulation of its container. It will also absorb the flavour of adjacent substances or vapours. Indeed, if a snuff of one flavour is allowed to lie open beside one of another flavour, the ultimate result will be what a snuff blender once called " a proper nose-puzzler."

The more usual shapes of snuff-boxes, old and new, are oval, round, square and oblong, though eccentricities of shape once were as usual as they were amusing. In Napoleon's day, for instance, there was almost a spate of boxes shaped like the Emperor's well-known hat. These were used mainly, and often on the sly, by pro-Bonapartists In this country boxes have been made in the shape of ladies' shoes, casks, bellows, horses' hooves, foxes' heads and the like.

ECCENTRIC SNUFF-BOXES

Messrs. G. Smith and Sons hold several "eccentrics" among their collection. One, which is probably unique, is in the form of a small, thick book—a real book—titled appropriately "Crumbs of Comfort," with a rectangular hollow cut in the middle of the pages to receive snuff. Another in the same collection is a little, macabre-looking coffin. Yet another, of which the firm is proud, is a silver box which once belonged to Sir John Wolfe Barry, one of the two designers of the Tower Bridge. These are but a few from the collection in the old shop in the Charing Cross Road.

Eccentricity was once shown, not only in shapes of, but in the materials used for the boxes. No doubt many of them did not stand up to investigation, but they had a pseudo-sentimental value nevertheless. Thus, there there were boxes made from the planks of Nelson's flagship, *Victory*, and from the table on which Wellington wrote his Waterloo dispatch. The desk of Mrs. Siddons, the famous actress, also contributed to the list. Even Shakespeare's mulberry tree in his garden at New Place, Stratford-on-Avon, came into it. The tree, so the story goes, was pulled down by a much later tenant of Shakespeare's house because he was tired of showing it to adoring visitors! This gave a local wood-worker, William Sharpe, his chance to make snuff-boxes from suitable bits of the tree which he had bought. An old line engraving of one of his boxes shows the lid carved with a mulberry sprig in fruit, and with Shakespeare's head on a bole at the side. There must have been some doubts cast on the genuineness of these boxes, for William Sharpe found it necessary to testify on oath as to the veracity of his sales-talk, an oath which he again registered on his deathbed.

The tenant referred to was a parson, the Reverend Francis Gastrell, who does not appear to have been a particularly pleasant gentleman. Not only did he lop down the tree, but later pulled down the whole house in revenge for the taxation he had to pay on it during his various absences.

REGENCY NOSES

The virtues expected in a good snuff-box were several, but, strangely, beauty of design was not the foremost of them. Nor, within reason, was its intrinsic worth. Snuff-taking was a serious matter in those days, and even the fops, despite their elegant display of ornate boxes, at least expected the latter to keep the snuff in good condition. The Regency noses and palates were not attuned to anything otherwise. Snuff came first, which was not remarkable when a man was often judged by the condition of the snuff he offered, perhaps a score of times a day, to his various acquaintances who, on their side, knew a good snuff when they sniffed it.

An elementary demand upon the snuff-box was (and is) that its lid should fit perfectly. Boxes ideal in this respect were not so common as one might imagine. Then, as now, it needed but a slight intake of air to " dull the edge " of a fine snuff. Even though no snuff escaped when the closed box was tapped on the back of the hand, there was still the possibility of air infiltration.

It must be emphasised that the above has little or no bearing on the modern snuff-box which is made with all the advantages of precision tools such as were not always available to the earlier makers.

One of the essentials of a well-fitting lid was a good hinge; and this brings us to one of the most engaging aspects of the snuff-box—the hinge. In handling a box there is a tendency for one to take this for granted, and not to examine it minutely. Sad as this omission may be, it is very prevalent; yet the hinges on many good boxes are exquisite in appearance and amazing in their performance. You may find the hinge of a gold box consisting of perhaps twenty tiny gold rollers, working on an invisible pin of the same metal. So finely made and fitted are these rollers that you can hardly distinguish one from its fellow. But one need not look only into rare boxes to see examples of hinge craftsmanship. It can even be found in boxes of wood or even horn, though the hinges lack some of the fineness of those made of precious metals or ivory. A remarkable feature of many hinges is that they are not made separately and *fitted*. The rollers are part of the box and lid which, consequently, consist of two pieces only—the box and the lid.

AN INVENTIVE SCOT

There was once great difficulty in making wooden boxes airtight, owing to the fitting of the hinge and, regarding this, there came into being a romantic story, the story of the Lawrencekirk snuff-box. A disabled, elderly Scot lived in the Highland village of that name. He was James Sandy, and rather a character in the village despite his being unable to leave his bed. He was a sort of Leonardo da Vinci of his little world, except that he did not paint! He was of an inventive turn of mind, and invented many strange and workable contraptions in addition to the snuff-box hinge he invented for wooden boxes. His hinge consisted of a series of rollers working on a fine brass rod. They were seven in number, three of them working independently and the others being part of the wooden box. He made boxes himself, into which he incorporated his hand-carved hinge. Soon they were copied far and wide, and it is often difficult, in examining snuff-box hinges, to say to what extent his principles have been copied. Happily, Sandy was indifferent to this, and lived to a ripe old age, cheerfully fashioning his snuff-boxes and anything else which came into his mind. A very interesting account of his life is given in Hone's *Table Book*, 1817, which, naturally, is fairly " hard to come by."

Pictures and portraits painted on snuff-boxes have put the latter into the higher realms of Art, and often account for the high prices obtained for them. Many distinguished artists have contributed to the " snuff-box picture gallery," among them the French Fragonard and the English Cosway. Cosway, a Devonshire man, born in 1740, became a Royal Academician and one of the foremost of English miniaturists. There are many examples of his work in Windsor Castle, as a result, no doubt, of his appointment in 1785 as principal painter to a fellow snuff-taker, the Prince of Wales, later George IV. Boxes illuminated by him fetch exceedingly high prices.

From Cosway we may come down the scale to hack artists, ever ready to turn the honest penny by " knocking off " hunting scenes and the like. Between Cosway and them there were always artists—some of them of repute—willing to paint the most erotic subjects on snuff-boxes, especially those with false bottoms or double inner tops. At one time snuff-box sellers were actually expected to have something of the kind " under the counter."

PORCELAIN BOXES

The finest painted boxes came from France, as can be testified by the major collections here and in America. Many of them proclaim that they were made more for the cause of Art than Utility. This can hardly be said of English gold snuff-boxes—mostly Georgian—which have a certain robustness about them suggesting they were made for a certain amount of wear and tear. They were generally engraved or chased, in contrast to the delicately enamelled and painted French examples.

Porcelain boxes are a *genre* of their own, and have long been out of use in this country. They were once popular among the foppish aristocracy, and usually came from France, which recalls the story of the gay Lord Petersham.

He was a great dandy of his time, a snuff-box collector and a friend of Beau Brummell. Someone was admiring his snuff-box, a delicate affair of Sèvres.

"Yes, it's a nice box for the summer," answered his lordship with detachment, " but it would never do for winter use."

George IV went one better. He had separate snuffs and boxes for morning, afternoon and night.

The sublimity of porcelain in its relation to snuff is to be found in the ancient snuff-bottles of China, many of which found their way to the Continent and England. The Portuguese introduced snuff to China in the seventeenth century, whereupon the Chinese were soon making snuff-bottles of great beauty and ingenuity. Not only were these of artistic exterior, but painted exquisitely *inside* as well. We are told that the painters worked lying on their backs, with brushes held between their teeth.

Examples of these Chinese bottles may be found in various English collections, among which are the Wallace Collection, and that at the Victoria and Albert Museum. Indeed, anyone wishing to see the most exquisite examples of snuff-boxes of all periods should visit these rewarding places.

It is amusing to reflect that when the price of snuff was a " consideration " a good deal of snuff-pilfering occurred. So much so that some of the larger boxes, of the " table " variety, were fitted with combination locks as a safeguard against servants, or perhaps even against the pilfering guest. Mary Lamb, sister of Charles Lamb (of *Essays of Elia* fame) was a relentless pilferer. She would leave their home in the Temple in the morning with an empty box and return with it in the evening full of snuff. Her method was, when offered snuff, to take a full pinch and put most of it surreptitiously into her own capacious box. But then, as we know, poor Mary was afflicted with the insanity which lurked in the family of her brother and herself.

A somewhat more ingenious pilferer was the famous eighteenth century French comedian, Scaramouche, who, during his recurring lean periods, regularly helped himself to large pinches of anyone else's snuff, re-selling the resultant mixture to a snuff-shop under the name of *Tabac de Mille Fleurs*—the Snuff of a Thousand Flowers.

"ON THE HOUSE"

Apart from the personal, pocket snuff-boxes there are the table varieties, many in the form of Scotch " mulls." These are usually made of whole rams' horns, maintaining the original twist which nature gave them, and fitted with a silver snap lid of exquisite craftsmanship. At one time such boxes were often found on the smoking-room tables of old inns in the North Country and, of course, Scotland. They were kept filled with good snuff by the landlord, the snuff being " on the house " both to customers and chance callers. There are still some magnificent specimens of mulls to be met with, though some possible change in the public's discrimination between *meum* and *teum* has ended the old and friendly practice mentioned above.

There are also pocket mulls, made from the tips of the horns only, but they have a tendency to be a little too unwieldy for modern dress.

To collect rare snuff-boxes is mainly a hobby for the well-to-do, but great pleasure may come from possessing a variety of quite good boxes picked up here and there. Indeed, many a true snuff-taker of today has up to a dozen or so boxes in silver, rosewood, horn, pewter, papier-mâché and the rest, bringing them out for an individual airing now and then.

We may also meet men with a fondness for the truly modern boxes now made in many graceful forms. Smith's of

Charing Cross Road specialise in these, and display boxes of all sizes and shapes made of gold, silver, Cornish pewter, horn and rosewood.

So the would-be modest collector of today is never at a loss in finding boxes of charm, both old and new.

Top: A fine snuff-box in modern engine-turned Silver

Middle: The work of modern craftsmen in French Rosewood

Below: A Pewter box, its lid stamped with an old die once used to decorate gunpowder-flasks

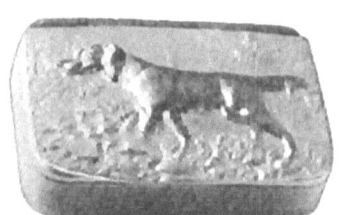

An early caricature of snuff-taking ladies

CHAPTER VII

Snuff-taking Ladies

> "*With Snuff the beauteous Celia shades her face,*
> *And adds a foil to every obvious grace.*
> *Her lips, o'erspread with dusky Vigo, speak*
> *The brighter colour of her lovely cheek.*"
> ARBUCKLE: *Poem on Snuff.* 1719.

SNUFF-TAKING, once so ostentatious, even flamboyant, is today mainly unobtrusive. It lends itself well to indulgence on the sly. The quiet man sitting next to you in the bus may well have a box of Golden Cardinal tucked away in his vest pocket. The magistrate who fines you for parking may well have taken an un-noticed pinch of Town Clerk while listening to your solicitor, and the parson, whose sermon you have just heard—with profit, we hope—may have returned deservedly to a neat little box of Spanish in his vestry desk. Even that pretty young girl whose averted eye you nearly caught in the park, may have in her handbag a diminutive box of Lavender or Lemon.

Be all this as it may, none of the examples is out of the question; certainly not that of the young lady, for snuff-taking by women is decidedly on the increase. Nor is this increase composed of women of any particular class or age; it ranges from the titled to the teen-aged.

Although snuff has this accepted feminine following, women are often delightfully furtive about it. When they purchase what is probably their first snuff-box it is for a gentleman friend, or, when they buy a certain blend of snuff, it is often because "he" likes it. But the average man behind the counter can generally see through their innocent ruse without the blink of an eye-lid. Strangely, women do not always go for the lighter, perfumed snuffs, but ask for one of the heavier, fruitier kinds.

Just when and where they take their fragrant pinch is something of a mystery. But they certainly buy it. You will, however, see the snuff-box produced freely by women in various circles in Soho, Chelsea and such Bohemian quarters.

There is a hint of the logical in women taking snuff, for it was a woman—Catherine de Medici—who was the first of her sex to take snuff in Europe, as we have read earlier. It was given to her by one, Jean Nicot, whose name, not without reason, is firmly fixed in the history of tobacco. He was of the French aristocracy and was France's Ambassador to Portugal. It was on an occasion of his return from Portugal and Spain, as related in a previous chapter, that he presented some dried tobacco leaves to Catherine. Some of these she used medicinally, as was customary in Spain, but she could not resist the method of which she had heard, of powdering the dried leaves and snuffing up *la poudre*. It pleased her, as it was to please so many of her sex through the next two centuries. We are speaking now of France, for, during the earlier period of snuff-taking in that country, England was calmly smoking her pipe.

"OLD SNUFFY"

But the time was soon to come, as we read elsewhere, when England turned to snuff in a big way, with queens indulging in it as heartily as the wenches in the Restoration plays did before them. The first eminent woman to write her name on the scroll of English women snuff-takers was Queen Charlotte, the wife of George III. She took snuff in such quantities as to make strong men turn pale at the thought of it. The Prince of Wales (later George IV), the Duke of York and her other sons rarely referred to her other than as "Old Snuffy." "Perhaps this was more for fun than from intentional disrespect," wrote Steinmetz, that indefatigable writer on tobacco of a century ago, "that the Queen was so designated. The etiquette of Courts is the most intolerable of all thraldoms, and none are so glad to escape from it as courtiers and princes themselves. Doubtless it was partly because she found the bondage of etiquette so intolerable that Queen Charlotte snuffed; and her sons, in calling her 'Old Snuffy', may have been influenced by a similar motive."

"Old Snuffy's" daughter-in-law, Caroline, was also a great snuff-taker. She married the Prince of Wales, mentioned above, and duly became Queen Caroline when her husband succeeded his father as George IV. He, like his mother, was a prodigious snuffer, though he introduced more *finesse* into his habit than did she. There had grown up a great—not to say fancy—ritual in snuff taking at that time. Thus, a snuff which George found acceptable in the morning was not suitable for the afternoon, and the afternoon snuff was jettisoned for the evening snuffing. It was said of him that he always had a dozen different kinds of snuff in elegant snuffboxes placed on the dinner-table with the wine.

No wonder, then, that Caroline developed a partiality for the magic dust. But there were probably more reasons than that for the unfortunate queen seeking some antidote to the blows Fate delivered her as soon as she married the Prince Regent. She was formally separated from her husband a year later, immediately after giving birth to a Princess (also a Charlotte). For a time she lived quietly in England, after which she betook herself to Italy, only to return to fight the accusations hinted at when her name was removed from the Prayer Book. Next, George sought a Bill of Divorce, alleging infidelity (as though he could expect anything else!). But she was defended at the bar of the House by one of the most eminent lawyers of the country—Lord Brougham—and the

Bill was thrown out, much to the delight of the populace, who thought more of her than of George, snuff-boxes and all.

A BAD LOT?

But the acrimonies did not end there. George III died at last, old and more than senile, and the Coronation of George IV took its place in what are today called "forthcoming events." Automatically, Caroline had become the Queen Consort and, presumably, had a right to be at the Coronation. But George had her forcibly expelled, no doubt to the satisfaction of his various high-born mistresses, including the celebrated Mrs. Fitzherbert. George was handsome and courtly, and among his wide circle was known as "the first gentleman in Europe." But he was a bad lot to everyone else, including his father, his wife, his children and his people. No wonder Caroline turned to the continual use of snuff, the "solace of nose and palate," and, in this case, perhaps, of the heart.

If we are really compelled to say anything good about the First Gentleman of Europe, it is this: the snuff he favoured most was a mixture of Rappee, perfumed with the elegant attar of roses, a compound which survives today as the popular Prince's Mixture. (This and many other snuffs are described in the chapter Varieties of Snuff.)

Alexander Pope, the satirical, amusing and accomplished poet of Queen Anne's reign and after, was a great snuff-taker. In his long, entertaining and satirical poem, "The Rape of the Lock," he makes his charming heroine, Belinda, repel an over-ardent suitor by flicking a good pinch of snuff in his face, which is one more proof that there was nothing unusual about a young lady carrying her own snuff-box around with her:

> "But this bold Lord, with manly strength endued,
> She with one finger and a thumb subdued;
> Just where the breath of life his nostrils drew,

A charge of snuff the wily virgin threw;
The Gnomes direct, to every atom just,
The pungent grains of titillating dust;
Sudden with starting tears each eye o'erflows,
And the high dome re-echoes to his nose."

Another amusing example of snuff-taking by ladies concerns the half-sister of Richard Steele, playwright, essayist and editor, a contemporary of Pope. He was a great snuff-taker, and so was his half-sister Jenny, despite the fact that she was a blue-stocking. The time came when she was about to be married, and custom demanded that she should take advice from Steele especially on the matter of snuff-taking. As a snuff-taker himself, he said, he was willing to allow the habit, if it were done with cleanliness, adding that he thought it desirable that she should not continue to have her nose all over snuff in future.

A FAMOUS WILL

But the greatest woman snuff-taker of all time was surely Margaret Thompson, whose name will last as long as any records of snuff-taking are kept. She was a Londoner, and lived in Boyle Street, a street which still exists in the purlieus of fashionable Mayfair. So great was her love of snuff that her purpose was never to be without it live *or dead.* Her last will and testament (1777) tells the story:

"In the name of God. Amen.

I, MARGARET THOMPSON, etc., being of a sound mind, etc., do desire that when my soul is departed from this wicked world, my body and effects may be disposed of in the following manner, etc.

I also desire that all my handkerchiefs that I may have unwashed at the time of my decease, after they have been got together by my old and trusty servant, SARAH STEWART, be put by her, and by her alone, at the bottom of my coffin, which I desire may be made large enough for that purpose, together with such a quantity of the best Scotch snuff (in which she knoweth I always had the greatest delight) as will cover my deceased body; and this I desire, and more especially as it is usual to put flowers into the coffins of departed friends, and nothing can be so pleasant and refreshing to me, as that precious powder; But I strictly charge that no one be suffered to approach my body till the coffin is closed, and it necessary to carry me to my burial, which I order in the following manner:—

Six men to be my bearers, who are well-known to be great snuff-takers in the parish of St. James's, Westminster; and instead of mourning, each to wear a snuff-coloured beaver, which I desire to be bought for that purpose, and given to them; Six Maidens of my old acquaintance to bear my pall, each to wear a proper hood, and to carry a box filled with the best Scotch snuff, to take for their refreshment as they go along. Before my corpse I desire that the minister may be invited to walk, to take a certain quantity of snuff, not exceeding one pound, to whom also I bequeath five guineas on condition of his doing so. And I also desire my old and faithful servant, Sarah Stewart, to walk along before the corpse to distribute every twenty yards a large handful of Scotch snuff on the ground, and to the crowd who may possibly follow me to the burial place—on condition I bequeath her £20. And I also desire that at least two bushels of the said snuff shall be distributed at the door of my house in Boyle Street.

I desire, also, that my funeral shall be at twelve o'clock at noon. And in addition to the various legacies I have left my friends in a former will, I desire that each person there shall be given a pound of the best Scotch snuff, as it is the grand cordial of human nature."

SNUFF SIGNS

Much good snuff came out of Scotland in those days, a fact which is of particular note. The Scots were so identified with snuff-taking that the carved figure of a kilted Highlander helping himself to a pinch of snuff was frequently seen as a sign outside tobacconists' doors to denote the sale of snuff within. These signs were not confined to Scotland, but were often seen in England and Ireland. Some of them were magnificent to behold, being carved life-size in wood, and painted in natural colours. Even today one may occasionally come across one, while in the window of Smith's shop stands a smaller version of the brawny Scot.

These tobacco- and snuff-sellers' signs took several amusing forms, and one wonders where they can all be, for they have virtually disappeared. One represented a negro's head, another a chubby black boy. Thus, one of the quacks mentioned in Chapter VIII advertised that his wonderful snuff could be obtained at the Sign of the Black Boy without Bishopsgate. Another of these " statue " signs took the form of a tall, commanding woman, taking a pinch of snuff. One of these is in the possession of Messrs. J. & H. Wilson, of Sheffield, where a collection is on view.

CHAPTER VIII

Snuff and Health

> " *When vapours swim before the eyes,*
> *And cloud the dizzy brain,*
> *Snuff, to dispel the mists, applies*
> *It's quick enliv'ning grain.*"
> WEEKLY JOURNAL, 1761.

THERE was a time when denunciations of snuff were an outlet for the spleen of busybodies, cranks and self-styled reformers, and later in this chapter we shall read of a few of the attacks directed against snuff, even when it was being taken by English folk of both sexes in place of pipe-smoking. The virulence of these attacks knew no limit; yet snuff-taking went merrily on its way, and nobody seemed one whit the worse.

One might have expected that the present astonishing rise in the popularity of snuff would bring down upon it similar maledictions. But no. We have heard nothing of the kind.

The only doctors we have approached on the subject have answered with benevolent neutrality, or even commendation. Medicated snuffs, containing, as they do menthol and other recognised inhalents, are, of course, highly favoured by the medical profession, as well they might be. Such snuffs are pleasant to take, and have a comforting effect upon the membranes. They are in considerable demand, especially by those prone to catarrhal and similar complaints.

Here and there one meets doctors who, like plenty of

other folk, describe snuff-taking as a "dirty habit." This, of course, is rubbish, for snuff is as hygienic a preparation as is ever allowed into our accommodating system. A forthright woman of the writer's acquaintance once put the matter to a disparaging doctor so conclusively that he has probably not yet forgotten it. "Doctor," she said, "I see nothing worse about a pinch of snuff in the nose than a piece of ripe Stilton in the mouth."

Certainly snuff today is completely devoid of adulteration, and made in conditions of absolute cleanliness.

This was not always so, and in the eighteenth century there were many unscrupulous makers and vendors of snuff who would go to any lengths to increase their profits. Powerful perfumes covered a multitude of adulterations, particularly in the snuffs sold to the ordinary people. The upper classes paid for good snuff, and they got it. Here is a note from an old account of the times:

"It was not unusual to save the sweepings of tobacco shops and warehouses for the purpose of mixing snuff.... Portions of leaf adhere to the shoes from the floors of the warehouses, and these are scraped into receptacles for the purpose; it is never wasted, but is dried and ground down with all extraneous matter, to put into dark coloured, highly perfumed snuff." Another account speaks of the diseased livers of cows and pigs being dried and ground into snuff, while red lead and oxide of iron were added to increase pungency, to say nothing of ammonia as a flavouring and a 'sharpener'."

Large numbers of doctors today are whole-heartedly in favour of snuff as a decongestant, and it is generally reckoned to be a relief, if not actually a cure, for those unpleasant complaints, *sinusitis* and catarrh. Also recognised is the property of snuff to clear the head and alert the brain, thus giving a stimulus to the whole system. It has even been suggested that if more people took good snuff, there would be less resort to " pep-pills."

TO SNEEZE OR NOT TO SNEEZE?

One objection to snuff, and for the most part it is ill-founded, is that it puts one to the inconvenience of sneezing. Actually, when a snuff-box is passed round among a group of snuff-takers, it is unusual to hear a sneeze, unless some extra pungent snuff has been produced by one of the number. Sufferers from *sinusities* and the like may be assured that after they have persevered with snuff for a day or two the tendency to sneeze will have almost disappeared.

Another objection is that snuff is liable to leave brown marks on white handkerchiefs. This can be overcome by the use of " snuff handkerchiefs." Thus, at Smith's Snuff Shop one can obtain charming handkerchiefs of Irish linen with a Paisley or Polka-dot design in a wide variety of attractive colours.

For people who work in a dust-laden atmosphere, snuff-taking is a boon. As evidence of this, we may quote from a national morning newspaper of May, 1962:

" SNUFF TO MAKE THE POSTMEN SNEEZE:

Britain's new big glass and concrete Post Offices are palaces of chromium and shining door-knobs, but behind the scenes they are dust traps.

" Postmen have to take snuff to clear the dust from their noses, postmen complained yesterday. They demanded at the annual Post Office Workers' Conference in Bournemouth that the G.P.O. should instal dust extracting machines in all sorting offices.

" A Cardiff postman said: ' I've never known so many snuff-takers as there are in the Post Office. You see them at night in little corners, slipping around with their little boxes, trying the various brands to get rid of the dust.' "

"Inquiries showed that several of the men had been advised by their doctors to take snuff, and the others followed suit. The idea was not so much to induce sneezing, for, as mentioned above, a self-respecting nose soon gets used to the occasional pinch. What the snuff does is to brace up the mucous membranes of the nose and sinuses, and to keep the mucous flow at a normal level, thus eliminating the deposits of dust."

Another pertinent item of news appeared in the morning and evening newspapers at about the same time. A prominent M.P., 60-years old Sir Godfrey Nicholson (of Gin fame) made a parachute drop over the sea "for fun," as he put it. An evening paper asked: " Was he sneezing after his dousing in the sea?" Certainly not. Sir Godfrey boasts that he has not had a cold for 10 years and puts down his immunity to taking snuff."

Many snuff-takers make the same claim, which seems to be supported by the fact that workers in snuff factories and shops are remarkably free from colds, owing no doubt, to their breathing snuff all their working hours.

WITCH-HUNTS

Such facts are commended to those doctors of today who indulge in sporadic witch-hunts in the Press, with snuff as their quarry.

The extent to which some of the old-time leeches denounced snuff knew no limit. Some even declared that, after death, the brains of snuff-takers were seen to be dried to mere membranes, and clogged with soot. They said they had made this discovery by examining the heads of executed criminals—they were not difficult to get in those days—who had been great snuffers.

It would make dismal reading to list more of the dire consequences of taking snuff as told by members of a fraternity who regularly carried canes with perforated gold, silver or ivory knobs containing snuff, " the great disinfectant." So we will take a look at some more cheerful observations on the health value of the fragrant pinch.

"During the reign of the cholera," says one, " smokers and snuff-takers were almost exempt from the disease . . . . How great then must be the utility of snuff! In a sick room it is manifest that smoking could not be altogether proper, but no objection could be urged against the grateful pinch of snuff. With snuff the physician defies the power of contagion . . . . In the combats which we have to sustain with those animals (germs), in a hundred forms, with a hundred names, which attack our bodies in a hundred different ways, which fix upon their prey and never quit it, but die surrounded by the trophies of their victories—but die in multiplying—tobacco in any form is a sovereign remedy. Snuff is fatal to insects."

The supporters of snuff in its hey-day, as we have said, went into their subject seriously, and, bearing in mind their lack of present-day statistics and high-powered analyses, did their job very well. They recorded that in the case of headaches, snuff " promoted a relieving secretion and facilitated respiration by the nose." They also said that it cured " the undue flowing of tears," adding " hence the notion that snuff improves the sight." They also claimed it as a cure for deafness, " ridding the Eustachian tube of the mucosities which obstruct it."

Another use of snuff, not generally known, was as a dentifrice. It was the custom to mix it with charcoal and myrrh, whereupon it became the " finest tooth-powder in the world." A further recipe was a mixture of salt, sugar and a pinch of snuff. For the guidance of anyone trying this today we would add that the pinch of snuff should be kept to a minimum. We have tried it!

In an age of quacks it was not surprising that snuff was

well exploited. There was "Grimstone's Eye Snuff," for instance, which was "most sovereign for clearing the head of all humours, and strengthening the sight." There was also the Imperial Snuff of a gentleman named Samuel Major. In an adroit advertisement in the *General Advertiser* of June 21, 1749, he even claimed his Imperial Snuff as a cure for insanity: "It hath set a great many to rights that was never expected, but there is but few, or none, that careth to have it published they were a little out of their senses, although it really be an ailment which none can help." There was more of it, but perhaps the above extract will suffice to end our chapter!

CHAPTER IX

Snuff in Story and Song

AN ANTHOLOGY

"THE puzzle of it is—to our mind—that no one has yet settled down to give us an anthology of snuff stories." These words appeared in a collectors' magazine a short time ago. True enough, there is no such anthology; nor can this short chapter fill the void, presenting, as it does, only a few examples of what might be in such an anthology, did it exist. Much of the amusing matter written about snuff is in verse of widely differing merit. Verse and worse, as one might say. Therefore, in the following collection will be found both stories and verse from a variety of publications.

In a foregoing chapter, *A Guide to Snuffs*, mention is made of a snuff called Irish High Toast, with a note that it has an amusing story behind it. Here is the story as told in a faded, pocket-size book written in 1832 which (the non-historically minded may care to know) was in the reign of William IV. The title is *Nicotiana: or the Smoker's and Snuff-taker's Companion*. The author is given as Henry James Mellor, Esq., but just who the gentleman was is not disclosed. Evidently he was of some little importance, for the " Esq." was used more selectively then than now.

The story, told differently, appears in several old books, but we choose this version as casting a side-light on the Englishman's one-time insistence on calling every Irishman Paddy, and making him say " begorrah " at frequent intervals. Not that either is done by Henry James Mellor, Esq., but because his true-born conception of the Irishman coincides so closely with the old tendency.

"Lundy Foot, the celebrated snuff manufacturer, had his premises at Essex-bridge, in Dublin, where he made the common scented snuffs then in vogue. In preparing the snuffs, it was usual to dry them in a kiln at night, which kiln was always left in strict charge of a man appointed to regulate the heat, and see the snuffs were not spoilt. The man usually employed in this business, Larey by name, a tight boy of Cork, chanced to get drunk over the "cratur," (i.e. a little whiskey) that he had gotten to comfort him, and quite regardless of his watch, fell fast asleep, leaving the snuff drying away. Going his round in the morning, Lundy Foot found the kiln still burning, and its guardian lying snoring with the fatal bottle, now empty, in his right hand. Imagining the snuff quite spoilt, and giving way to his rage, he instantly began belabouring the shoulders of the sleeper with the stick he carried.

"Och, be quiet wid ye, what the devil's the matter, master, that ye be playing that game," shouted the astounded Larey, as he sprang up and capered about under the influence of the other's cane.

"You infernal scoundrel, I'll teach you to get drunk, fall asleep and suffer my property to get spoilt," uttered the manufacturer, as each word was accompanied by a blow across the dancing Larey's shoulders.

"Stop! stop! wid ye now; sure you wouldn't be after spaking to ye'r old sarvant that way—the snuff's only a little dryer, or so, may be," exclaimed the "boy" trying to soften matters.

"You big blackguard, you, didn't you get drunk and fall asleep?" interrogated his master as he suspended his arm for a moment.

"Och, by all the saints, that's a good 'un now; where can be the harum of slaaping wid a drop or so; besides—but hold that shilelah—hear a man spake raison."

Just as Lundy Foot's wrath had in some degree subsided in this serio-comic scene, and he had given the negligent watcher his nominal discharge, who should come in but a couple of merchants. They instantly gave him a large order for the snuffs they were usually in the habit of purchasing, and requested to have it ready for shipping by the next day. Not having near so large a quantity by him, in consequence of what had happened, he related the occurrence to them, by way of illustration, pointing out the trembling Larey, occupied in rubbing his arms and back, and making all kinds of contortions.

Actuated by curiosity, the visitors requested to look at the snuff, although Lundy Foot told them, from the time it had been drying, it must be burnt to a chip. Having taken out the tins, they were observed to emit a burnt flavour, anything but disagreeable, and on one of the gentlemen taking a pinch up, and putting it to his nose, he pronounced it to be the best snuff he had ever tasted. Upon this, the others made a similar trial, and all agreed that chance had brought it to a degree of perfection before unknown.

Reserving about a third, Lundy Foot sold the rest to his customers. The only thing that remained now, was to give it a name: for this purpose, in a facetious mood, arising from the sudden turn affairs had taken, the master called his man to him, "Come here, you Irish blackguard, and tell these gentlemen what you call this snuff of your own making."

Larey, who did not want acuteness, and perceived the aspect of things, replied: "And is it a name ye'r in want of, Sir? Fait, I should have thought it was the last thing you couldn't give: without indeed, you've given all your stock to me already. You may even call it 'Irish Blackguard' stidd of one Michael Larey."

As many a true word is spoken in jest, so it was christened on the spot. The snuff was sent to England immediately, and to different places abroad, where it soon became such a favourite that the proprietor took out a patent and rapidly made a fortune.

Such are the particulars connected with the far-famed snuff, Lundyfoot or Irish Blackguard, (later—much later—to become known as Irish High Toast.)

The moral of this story is that, when you next buy Irish High Toast in the Charing Cross Road, you give a thought to Michael Larey, its great inventor. Alas, there is no way of knowing if Lundy Foot allowed him to profit commensurably from his discovery.

RABBIE BURNS' BOX

Robert Burns, like most good Scots of his day, took snuff in plenty. He was born right into the Snuff Age in 1759, but lived to enjoy his "fragrant pinch" only until 1796. His snuff-box still survives, however, carefully preserved in the Museum of the Society of Antiquaries of Scotland. During the poet's last years in Dumfries, his almost inseparable associate was a Mr. Bacon, who kept a lively hostelry near the town.

"Many a merry night did they spend together," says an old account, "over their cups of foaming ale or bowls of whisky toddy, and on some of these occasions Burns composed some of his best convivial songs. The bard and the innkeeper became so attached to each other that, as a token of regard, Burns gave Bacon his snuff-box, which for many years had been his pocket companion.

"The knowledge of this gift was confined to a few of their jovial brethren. But after Bacon's death in 1825 (he had outlasted Burns by nearly thirty years), when his household furniture was sold by public auction, this snuff-box was offered among other trifles, and someone in the crowd at once bid a shilling for it. There was a general exclamation that it was not worth twopence, and the auctioneer seemed about to knock it down. He first looked, however, at the lid, and then read in a tremendous voice the following inscription upon it: *Robert Burns, officer of the Excise*. Scarcely had he uttered the words, says one who was at the sale, before shilling after shilling was rapidly and confusedly offered for this relic of Scotland's great bard, the greatest anxiety prevailing; while the bidding rose higher and higher, till the trifle was finally knocked down for five pounds. The box was made of the tip of a horn, neatly turned round at the point; its lid is plainly mounted with silver, on which the inscription is engraved."

Some accounts say that the successful bidder later bequeathed it to his son who, in due course, presented it to the above Museum.

THE GIANT SNEEZE

The carelessness of inveterate snuff-takers is proverbial. Presumably it is because they are so transported with delight as to be regardless of appearances. Until a few years ago, the landlord of a famous City tavern always seemed to have a dim, brown haze about him, and he must have taken a pinch of snuff almost every five minutes of his day. No fuss; just a sly production of his box, and a sniff as surreptitious as the status of his immediate company might demand.

This brings us to a fairly recent story of an old Kensington gentleman, a snuff-taker and a true-to-typer. His upper lip was always stained with snuff, and a slap on his waistcoat would bring out a cloud of the brown powder. A friend once called upon him, accompanied by his dog, a giant great dane. The dane, no doubt ascertaining if there were any other dogs about, gave a powerful sniff at the carpet, and a moment later the room was shaken by what was probably the greatest sneeze in history, so great that it blew out the fire.

SAID THE PARSON . . .

From dogs to dog-collars is not a long step. Here is a very brief story of two clergymen in the reign of good Queen Anne (or any other monarch of your choice!)

"Brother A.," said one of the two clergymen, "Is it possible that you take snuff? Pray, give up the unseemly practice. It is alike unclerical and uncleanly. Snuff! Why, my dear brother, even a pig would turn away his nose from it!"

Brother A. mildly brought out his snuff-box and took a pinch, saying, "I suppose, of course, Brother B., you never take a pinch yourself?"

"No, indeed," exclaimed his friend with virtuous horror.

Another pinch, and Brother A. rejoined, "Then, dear brother, which is more like the pig—you or I?"

THIEF OF TIME

Among the oddities and curios reposing in a private drawer at Smith's is an old manuscript. It is yellowed and, in copperplate writing, sets forth relentlessly how much time a man may lose by his addiction to the social pinch. It is unsigned and un-dated, but we have encountered its depressing contents elsewhere, in an old volume which attributes the actuarial estimate to an early Lord Stanhope. This is how it goes:

"Every professed inverterate and incurable snuff-taker at a moderate computation, takes one pinch of snuff in ten minutes; every pinch with the agreeable ceremony of blowing and wiping his nose, and other incidental circumstances consumes two minutes and a half out of every ten, allowing sixteen hours to a snuff-taker's day, this amounts to two hours and twenty-five minutes of every natural day, and one day out of every ten. One day out of ten amounts to thirty-six days and a half in a year. Hence, if we suppose the practice to be persisted in forty years, two entire years of a fashionable snuff-taker's life will be dedicated to tickling his nose and two more to blowing it! And, if the expense of snuff, snuff-boxes and handkerchiefs were considered it would be found this luxury encroaches as much on his Income, as it does on his Time."

So now we know!

THE ADMIRAL'S SHIRT

Admiral Sir Charles Napier liked his snuff as well as did Lord Nelson. They were contemporaries, though Nelson was some twenty years older, and Napier's main exploits did not take place until after the Battle of Trafalgar. He achieved great success when in charge of the Portuguese Fleet, a success he did not repeat when he led the Baltic Fleet twenty years later. It was in this connection that he was supposed to have said he would be in Cronstadt or hell within a month. His somewhat abject failure was responsible for a comment made later, that, had the Government stopped the supply of snuff before he went to the Baltic, and he had had news that there was a good supply of snuff in Cronstadt, the result might have been different.

Old Charlie, as he was affectionately called, was in the habit of buying his snuff in Bristol, and, according to the *Naval and Military Gazette*, went to a curious expedient when going to replenish his supplies with no money in his pocket. It occurred at his usual shop, but there was a man behind the counter who did not know him, and declined to trust him to "come back later."

"I am Admiral Sir Charles Napier," explained the old sea-dog."

"And how am I to know that you're anything of the sort?" asked the tradesman.

"Dammit, man, I tell you who I am, and you won't believe me," snapped Napier. "Give me the packet at once."

"No, sir, not unless you pay me."

What the Admiral did next has a Churchillian flavour about it. He "suddenly thought of convincing proof; and, unbuttoning, he hauled out the tail of a nether garment, and, turning it over, triumphantly pointed out the name—'Charles Napier, R.N.'"

He got his snuff.

It says much for snuff that over a couple of centuries it inspired poets of low and high degree to write of it, sometimes in praise and sometimes in satire. A few examples of both will be found in the following pages. We may start with an extolling poem by no other than James Boswell, Dr. Johnson's companion and biographer. Apart from these two pre-occupations, what else he did was his own affair, but he left enough notes behind to show that privately he warmed both hands at the fire of life. In his book, "Shrubs of Parnassus," he placed this little poem in praise of snuff (which is not surprising when we remember that Dr. Johnson went about with his waitcoat pockets full of snuff):

> "Oh Snuff! our fashionable end and aim!
> Strasburgh, Rappee, Dutch, Scotch! whate'er thy name;
> Powder celestial! Quintessence divine!
> New joys entrance my soul while thou art mine,
> Who takes—who takes thee not! Where'er I range
> I smell thy sweets from Pall Mall to the 'Change.
> By thee assisted, ladies kill the day,
> And breathe their scandal o'er their tea;
> Nor less they prize thy virtues when in bed,
> One pinch of thee revives the vapoured head,
> Removes the spleen, removes the qualmish fit,
> And gives a brisker tone to female wit,
> Warms in the nose, refreshes like the breeze,

> Glows in the head, and tickles in the sneeze.
> Without it, Tinsel, what would be thy lot!
> What, but to strut neglected, and forgot!
> In vain thy dress, in vain thy trimmings shine,
> If the Parisian snuff-box be not thine.
> Come to my nose, then snuff, nor come alone,
> Bring taste with thee, for taste is all thy own."

The above, of course, is a classic in snuff literature.

SATIRE

However bitter satire may be, it rarely fails to be amusing. An example of this crops up in an old copy (1807) of the *European Magazine*. It is a fairly lengthy tirade against snuff, so we will be content with a couple of stanzas. The poem is really a mock comparison between the craze for snuff and the finer things of life:

> " Snuff's my delight! let other youths declare
> Their minds to Celia or to Chloe fair:
> Let them in sportive glee lead down the dance,
> And shyly steal the love-inspiring glance;
> Beauty and all its charms are foolish stuff,
> If you compare it to a pinch of snuff.
>
> No more let music pour its soothing strain,
> Or teach in echoes mountains to complain;
> Enrapt the soul with soft melodious thrill,
> And make the senses act against the will;
> Say, can it equal with its power divine,
> The pleasing sound of " Take a pinch of mine!"

PANDORA'S BOX

In 1719 there appeared a clever skit on " the prime habit of the day." It was entitled *Pandora's Box; a Satyr against Snuff,* and it caused considerable stir at the time. Here is an extract from it:

> .... " now, 'tis by every sort
> And sex adored, from Billingsgate to Court,
> But ask a wench, ' how oysters sell?'—if nice,
> She begs a pinch before she sets a price.

Go thence to 'Change, inquire the price of Stocks;
Before they ope their lips they open first the box.
Next pay a visit to the Temple, where
The lawyers live, who gold to heaven prefer;
You'll find them stupified to that degree,
They'll take a pinch before they take their fee."

PLEASURES OF SNUFF-TAKING

As a " counterblaste " (as James I would have put it) to the above scarifying verses, here is a poem of praise. Doggerel, it is true, but nevertheless doggerel from the heart:

Let some the joys of Bacchus praise,
The vast delights which he conveys,
    And pride them in their wine;
Let others choose the nice *morceau,*
The piquant joys of feasting know,
    But other gifts are mine.
Oh where shall I for courage fly?
Or what restorative apply?
    A pinch be my resource;
Perchance the French are not polite,
And with my country wish to fight,
    Then I must grieve perforce.
To soothe the mind in such an hour,
A pinch of snuff has ample power;
    One pinch—all's well again!
A pinch of snuff delights again,
And makes me view with great disdain,
    And soothes my patriot grief.
Thus for the list of human woes,
The pangs each mortal bosom knows,
    I find in snuff relief;
It makes me feel less sense of sorrow,
When modern bards their verses borrow,
    And soothes my patriot grief.
Then let me sing the praise of snuff,
Give me, ye gods, I pray, enough;
    Let others boast their wine;
Let some prefer the nice *morceau,*
And piquant joys of feasting know,
    The bliss of snuff be mine.

SIMPLICITY

Here is a piece of verse by the Rev. Willian King (1788) which at least has simplicity on its side. It is the source of the two lines quoted at the head of our Introduction.

". . . . before I budge an inch
I hail Aurora with a pinch;
After three cups of morning tea
A pinch most grateful is to me.
If I on ancient classics pore,
Or turn their learned pages o'er,
I take a pinch at every pause,
A tribute of my just applause.
Whene'er I dip in page historic,
Or pass an hour in wit with Yorick,
I relish more each paragraph
If seasoned with a pinch and laugh.
Or, if discussing subjects curious,
I revel in a pinch luxurious;
E'en joyous friends and claret rosy
Insipid are *sans* pinches cosy.
Whate'er I do, where'er I be,
My social box attends on me;
It warms my nose in winter's snow,
Refreshes midst midsummer's glow;
Of hunger sharp it dulls the edge,
And softens grief as some alledge.
Thus, eased of care or any stir,
I broach my freshest canister;
And freed from trouble, grief or panic,
I pinch away in snuff balsamic.
For rich or poor, in peace or strife,
It smooths the rugged path of life."

MY NOSE

In Miss Sheridan's annual *Comic Offering* for 1834 appeared that smart little verse *To My Nose*. It was attributed to "the talented artist-author, Alfred Crowquill."

Knows he that never took a pinch,
Nosey, the pleasure thence which flows?
Knows he the titillating joys

>   Which my nose knows?
>   O nose! I am as proud of thee
>   As any mountain of its snows;
>   I gaze on thee, and feel that pride
>   A Roman knows!

There are many more examples of bardic wit which we could quote, but, with space on our heels, we must let the above little gem conclude the chapter—*and the book.*

INDEX

Addison, 31, 49
Amurath IV., Sultan, 21
Anne, Queen, 24, 25

Barham, Rev. H., 52
Barry, Sir J. Wolfe, 58
Bergerac, Snuff Museum, 54
Boswell, James, 85
Boyce, Sir Leslie, 51
Brimson, W. A., 50
Brougham, Lord, 67
Burns, Robert, 25, 81

Cadiz, 22
Caroline, Queen, 32, 67
Caroline, Queen, 31, 66
Charles II, 21, 28
Charles II, of France, 18
Charlotte, Queen, 32
Chartreux Fathers, 42
Christie's, 54
Churchill, Sir Winston, 50
Columbus, Christopher, 17, 19
Cosway, Richard, 61
Counterblaste to Tobacco, 28
Crown Street, 14
Crumbs of Comfort, 58

Danes, St. Clement, 51
Defoe, Daniel, 53
Devizes, 36
Dickens, Charles, 12, 15
Doughty Street, 12
Downing Street, 12
Drake, Sir Francis, 20, 23
Dryden, John, 31
Dulwich, 50

Ellis, J. Aytoun, 43

Fire, Great, 22
Fleet Street, 13
Foyle's Bookshop, 14
Fragonard, Jean, 61

Garaway's Coffee House, 31
Garrick, David, 31
Gawith Hoggarth & Co., Ltd., 38
George IV., 32, 50, 53, 68
Goldsmith, Oliver, 31
Grace, W. G., 51
Grimstone's Eye Snuff, 77

Hardham's, 12
Harrison, Thomas, 38
Havanas, 23
Hawkins, Sir John, 20
Hernandez, Francesco, 18
Hog Lane, 14
Hunt, Leigh, 49

Innocent, Pope, 20

James I, 21, 28
Jockey Club, 43
Johnson, Dr., 15, 30, 31

Keats, John, 31
Kendal, 34, 36

Lamb, Mary, 62
Lane, Ralph, 20
Lawrencekirk Boxes, 60
Lord's Pavilion, 51
Louis XIV, 11
Lundy Foot, 81

McCausland, Hugh, 35
Major Samuel, 77
Man's Coffee House, 31
Mary Queen of Scots, 27
Medici, Catherine de, 18
Mitcham, 36

Nando's Coffee House, 31
Napier, Admiral, 84
Napoleon, 32
Nash, Beau, 29
Nelson, Horatio, 55
Nicholson, Sir G., M.P., 75
Nicot, Jean, 18
No. 1 London, 12

Old Snuffy, 67

Pane, Romano, 17
Petersham, Lord, 61
Pewterers' Company, 56
Philip II, King, 18
Pitt, William, 56
Plague, Great, 21
Plymouth, 25
Pope, Alexander, 31, 68
Port St. Mary, 22, 23

Raleigh, Sir W., 17, 19, 28
Ransome, Arthur, 13
Reynolds, Sir Joshua, 31
Rooke, Admiral Sir G., 22
Royal Air Force, 48
Royal Fusiliers, 52

St. Paul's Cathedral, 52
San Domingo, 19
Sandy, James, 60
Scaramouche, 63
Seven Dials, 12
Shakespeare, William, 58
Sharpe, William, 58
Sheffield, 34, 36
Smith, George, 12
Smith's Snuff Shop, 14
Snuff Rasps, 26
Sotheby's, 11
Steele, Richard, 31, 69

Thompson, Margaret, 69
Tobago, 19
Tonquin Bean, 42

Urban VIII, Pope, 22

Victory, H.M.S., 58
Vigo, 23
Vigo Prize Snuff, 23
Virgina, 20

Walpole, Horace, 56
Wellington, Duke of, 58
Will's Coffee House, 31
Wilson, J. & H., Ltd., 39
Wilson's & Co. (Sharrow) Ltd., 39
Wren, Sir Christopher, 52

www.ingramcontent.com/pod-product-compliance
Lightning Source LLC
Chambersburg PA
CBHW021813220426
43662CB00006B/293